THE BATTLE OF BULIMIC BARB

By Barbara Noon

Ebook ISBN: 9781533166708

barbnoonbooks@yahoo.com

Cover Design: AshilleryDesign at Fiverr.com.

TABLE OF CONTENTS

CHAPTER ONE

PUTTING MY CHILDHOOD UNDER A MICROSCOPE

For thirty years I have been silent about my recovery from bulimia; I did not even want to think about this embarrassing illness. There was a fear that the disease would return if I allowed the subject of bulimia to enter my mind, so all memories of this disorder were blocked. My passions in life are fighting for animals' rights and a clean environment; not writing a book about vomiting! But one day I realized I had a rather unique experience in my life, and knew that writing a book about bulimia could help heal many people. This book contains advice that comes from my own experiences without being influenced by anyone else; I have refrained from reading any other books on bulimia before writing this for you.

I hope when you read the enormous amounts of food I ate and the patterns of behavior that took up my time, you will know that there is a good possibility you can be healed of this illness. Eating was never what was most important to me, yet it took over my life for eleven years, from age 19 until age 30. If you are like me, you do not want to focus on food; you want to be healthy and have fun, be successful and fit in, while still being unique. I enjoyed food, but never wanted it to rule my world. Yet, it did.

At 60 years of age, I can finally look back on the embarrassing situations from those eleven years and reflect on what happened to me. Sometimes the memories are amusing, and sometimes I wish I could go back in time and kick myself. Since I am not a professional or an expert, I will simply make suggestions that I would try if I went back in time. As you read my story, you can decide for yourself whether my bulimia was due to upbringing, life's disappointments, a habit, or a combination of all three.

One of the many items that bulimics wrestle with is, "Why would I, a young person with above-average intelligence and common sense, develop bulimia?" We cannot understand how such a "dumb illness" could happen to us when we can see through so many other problems. In order to understand bulimia fully, we need to find out what started the tendency toward a bulimic lifestyle.

My personality and experiences as a youngster may have led to an eating disorder. One of my main weaknesses was that I had no coping skills. My family did not argue as no bickering was allowed, and we rarely talked about anything but happy subjects. I had little stress and thought God was always smiling down on me. My childhood was spent in a sheltered world of goodness. My family lived in the same house until I was in my twenties and most of my friends did not move either, so my life was consistent, with friends I thought would be there forever. I planned to marry my grade school crush, become a gym teacher, and we would live on a farm where the pigs would smile and the sun would shine.

Even though my childhood was very happy, I cried at the drop of a hat if something went wrong in school, not knowing what else to do, and was quite a worrier. As a youngster, I was never punished severely, and ran around the neighborhood freely. I tended to overdo my enthusiasm. When disciplined kids would open a pack of gum, they would eat one piece and save the rest. I would jam piece after piece in my mouth until the pack was empty and I could barely chew! Everyone thought it was funny, but now I look suspiciously back on actions such as this, and wonder if it was a clue to the future! Let me be clear that I do not blame my parents one bit for my bulimia. Who wouldn't want to live in a household with no arguing, the freedom to run around the neighborhood, and a secure childhood! I had wonderful parents.

At age 13, I was very active, jogging almost a mile to school and back at lunchtime, but lunch consisted of four sugar sandwiches – toasted white bread with butter and sugar, sometimes with cinnamon added for variety. My dad was home at lunchtime, and proclaimed, "You're going to get fat, fat, fat!" Since we rarely said anything negative to each other, it really hurt my feelings, and I resented him for that blatant statement. Even with my strange eating habits, I stayed slim for a few more years due to all of my exercise. Nothing else was said about my sugar sandwich lunches and they continued to be my lunch, with some chocolate fudge added as a snack when I got home from school.

One step can lead to another, and I was in a progression toward an eating disorder. At age 16, I outgrew my dorky stage and became quite attractive. The good luck fairy had already blessed me with perfect pitch and a wonderful singing voice. I had a full but clear tone with a lyric soprano range (I could sing up to the "C" that is eight white keys below the highest note on the piano). The music director of the high school called me "Star," and it was assumed I would be a success throughout life.

Fig. 1

This is an old, poor-quality picture of me in 1972, pre-bulimia. I will be honest - it was fun being popular in a large high school, even though I never went out to parties or had a lot of friends. Singing, cheerleading, and acting in plays in school made me feel very special in my small world. But weight started to creep on. As a cheerleader, I weighed 116 pounds, but by my junior year of high school (a year after the cheerleader picture was taken), I gained 22 pounds and at 138 pounds, I could no longer hold in my stomach or hide the fullness in my face and neck. Even though the weight gained was not a huge amount, I felt embarrassed and heavy.

CHAPTER TWO

AN OBSESSION WITH FOOD BEGINS

My mother was on a very popular diet in the 70's, and I learned the diet from her. I studied the diet's rules with "legal and illegal foods" and "limited and unlimited vegetables." Taking this new regime seriously, I lost all my weight, and poured over the organization's diet magazines, reading about how other people lost weight and examining their before and after pictures. "Illegal" foods became synonymous with "sin" to me. Even after losing the weight, I just added more cereal and other "legal foods" in order to maintain my goal weight. This was a bit obsessive since the maintenance program allowed small portions of sweets and treats, but I could not even think of eating what I had come to believe were "illegal" foods. We used a small scale for food where I would weigh ounces of meat and cheese, as I had to be accurate in eating all my legal foods. I truly believed if I ate the wrong measurement of any food or consumed any "illegal" foods, I would become fat.

This diet company has changed a lot since those days, allowing much more variety and trade-off foods, and even though I see the old program as a start to some of my obsessive fears toward eating certain foods, the diet or company is not at fault. All of my problems came from my own head, and another person in the same situation following the same diet would not have ended up a bulimic. In fact, thousands of people have been successful on the diet and I think it is a wise program with a good variety of foods.

My obsessive behavior caused another tiff between Dad and me. At a relative's wedding reception, my strict food rules showed signs of the impending illness, but no one realized it at the time, including me. We were seated at one of the round guest tables, and my dad asked if I wanted something to drink. I requested a diet Sprite. He brought me what looked like a diet Sprite, but when I took a sip it tasted suspiciously sweet. I asked him if it was "diet," and he said they did not have diet Sprite so it was a regular Sprite. I pushed the glass away and angrily glared at him as if he were the worst person in the world! I was furious that he was not taking "how I had to eat and drink" seriously, and did not talk to him for the rest of the night, resenting him for years. Poor dad - I wish I could go back in time and treat him kinder.

At age 17, one event clouded life's sunshiny days. My childhood had been speckled with bouts of severe tonsillitis, and my parents decided my tonsils should be removed. I remember asking a very cold-mannered doctor at the hospital if getting my tonsils out would ruin my singing voice and explained to the doctor that if anything would change my voice, I did not want my tonsils removed. He insisted my voice would stay just the same. Weeks after the operation, those high notes were impossible to find, and the tone was altered. Some muscles were cut or tightened – to this day I do not know what happened, but something definitely affected my voice. For example, I could no longer reach back and put the tip of my tongue behind my uvula like I used to because my muscles were now too tight, my o's and oo's were not clear, and sometimes my voice cracked. Allergies set in for the first time, which may have been a side effect of the tonsillectomy. Frustration and fear quickly took over when the ease of singing left; my natural talent was gone.

Now, in truth, I never would have made a career out of opera or taught music because I wasn't crazy about opera, and music was not my passion, but losing that golden voice meant I no longer was special. Singing well had always been a part of my identity. It broke my heart to hear myself sing from then on, and quite often when I sang, I ended up in tears. It got to the point I could not complete one phrase of a song without choking up. The idea that I would be "great" was definitely gone. It may sound as if I was a very conceited individual, but I don't think I was to any extreme; we all want to like ourselves and see ourselves as unique in some way, and my gift was taken away by that tonsillectomy.

Not only was my singing voice ruined, but my days of being pretty and healthy were about to disappear. Around age 18, teenage acne finally took hold and did not disappear until age 53! Imagine how I felt starting college, with acne all over my face, including a "beard" of acne going around my jaw line. Pimples were on my back, chest, and occasionally there was acne on my arms and legs.

In pictures I usually looked fine, because I no longer allowed close ups. Almost every picture of me taken at close range during those years was destroyed, and recent pictures are snapped at a distance and then brought up close through modern editing so my scars do not show. The only picture I have to show my acne is the cover photo of this book. In case the acne was not noticed, I have a close up following this paragraph. This picture was from my early years with bulimia, before the tetracycline taken to try to help my acne gave me a gray line on my teeth and before the bottoms of my teeth wore down. My acne became worse than in this picture, because I lived through a few years with scabs nearly always on my face.

Fig. 2

My mother tried to help me by putting me on Accutane, an extremely strong medicine for fighting acne. Not too many people have been on Accutane four times, but I was and it greatly helped my acne. However, with my compulsive picking (making sure any oils or blockages were thoroughly out of my pores), my smooth face from childhood was becoming marred and scarred. This acne may have been genetic, hormonal, or it may have been from sensitivity to milk, of which I drank large amounts daily until age 53. There is a link between dairy and acne in some individuals, but I did not know this until recently. So you can see that the "perfect life" had fallen apart, and I was discouraged and embarrassed about how I looked.

CHAPTER THREE

COLLEGE YEARS – A LOSS OF DIRECTION

Attending college was anticlimactic after all those years of being a singer and cheerleader in high school. My first college was Central Michigan University in the middle of Michigan, and the two hour trip from Detroit was a boring drive of brown dirt and barren, flat land. Central was a good college for physical education majors, and I thought I was going to fulfill my dream of becoming a gym teacher. That was shattered when I was required to take a segment on basketball where a lot of large, rough girls were bumping into me on the basketball court. I had never played a real basketball game before, nor did I know the rules. I would say it was more like bumper cars without the cars! It was not fun and I was frightened on the court, and this made me think physical education may not be the right career path for me. It was upsetting not to have a clear direction, but from that moment on I was not sure what I wanted to do with my life.

Another change that comes with college is the cultural change. At that time in Michigan the legal drinking age was eighteen. The freshman dorm became a huge party on weekends, with empty beer cans lining the halls. I did not believe in drinking as I thought inebriated students looked sloppy and immature. Drinking was a waste of time and too many calories, so I did not agree with the mentality of most of the fellow students. The irony was that in a short while, I would be wasting my time and risking calories by binging and purging, yet I still held that I had better morals because I didn't believe in drinking or doing drugs!

I would see a lot of college girls getting drunk and being catty, yet they had boyfriends. It upset me greatly, but I think the only reasons I did not have a boyfriend were that I didn't socialize a lot, and there was that problem with acne. The other girls also had jobs and friends and could handle college. They accepted the career path they chose and all that comes with it. Looking around at the girls on campus, all busy with their social lives, I felt like I was below them and left out; I wanted to be part of the group, but I did not want to be like them.

With hindsight, I realize I could have been friendly to a lot of people at college, but I seemed to lack the insight that I could have casual friends who were not "just like me" without losing my own sense of self. I pined for the old times, where change never happened. Adulthood was a huge disappointment and the loss of direction took the rug out from under me.

The real change in my behavior occurred when I was eating three meals a day at the college cafeteria, and two on weekends. I worried about having only two meals a day on Saturday and Sunday, even though I always had snacks in my dorm. It was crucial for me to eat healthy foods, so I started stealing oranges from the cafeteria, hiding them in the pocket of my sweatshirt and in my hood! Needless to say, I was quickly caught and the lunch ladies had a talk with me. I remember saying, "But I have to have these oranges. I need them!" This is a sign of an obsession and eating disorder, but I did not think anything was wrong. I thought I was being intelligent by taking a healthy food that I needed and that they did not provide. They owed me those oranges, and three meals a day. This was the first time I ever stole anything, and it was just the start.

CHAPTER FOUR

BULIMIA BEGINS

The fateful day arrived – the day I became a bulimic. I was alone in my dorm room. Earlier, my roommate had offered me some small Heath bars from a box of candy, and of course, I declined. When she left to practice high jump, the urge to eat a Heath bar became unbearable! I picked up one Heath bar and took a bite. It was so sweet and delicious! I ate the entire small Heath bar, then, in total abandonment, I wiped off the top of the open Coke bottle my roommate had left, and took a swig. This was the first "illegal" food I had consumed in a couple of years. All of a sudden, it hit me like a ton of bricks: "What if I get fat?" Yes, one small Heath bar had me worried. Then it dawned on me that perhaps I could throw it up. I went into the bathroom, leaned over, tightened some stomach muscles, and it was all too easy. The Heath bar and Coke swig were brought up and flushed down the toilet. I was instantly hooked. Thus began eleven years of binging and purging - just like that.

I may not have been such a strong bulimic if I did not have this ability to purge without making any noise; there was no straining, no toothbrush or fingers down the throat. After awhile, I started to be proud of this accomplishment. Other bulimics were amateurs; they had to actually make throw up noises and gag, as they didn't have the technique and skill I possessed! Yes it is sad that my life skills had been reduced to "Best at vomiting." I also took pride that, "Mine is the worst case of bulimia, ever." I had to feel special somehow. Do not try to throw up just to see if you can. It is frightening to think that eleven years of binging and purging started with seeing if I could throw up a mini-Heath bar.

My life at college became a fog, with nothing working out and no niche for me. It is not as if bulimics do not try to live the life they want, as I did try many different avenues. My session with an academic counselor ended with me feeling that I was not career-worthy. I had looked into Wildlife Biology, but he counseled me that it was not a career for a woman, and fighting fires in the forest was out for the same reason. Two more careers checked off the list! (Back in my day, discrimination against women did influence choices.) I checked out books from the library on careers, but none of the options "sang to me." I was especially excited about the Ecology Club at Central, because I loved nature and considered a career in some form of conservation. Unfortunately, the Ecology Club was headed up by a 24 year old "forever student" who was more into philosophy than action. Every meeting was a long discussion, with large words. Government and economics were topics that were over my head and were his favorites, and I quickly became disillusioned. As an aside, the last day I spent in the group he had his T-shirt on backward, with the tag sticking out in the front.

"Backward Shirt" (I think his name was Tom) asked me to his apartment for dinner, and I never liked to hurt a person's feelings, so I accepted his invitation. I rode my bicycle about half a mile to his apartment and was brought into a living room with a coffee table and a couch. Tom suggested I sit on the floor in front of the coffee table. After a short wait, he brought out a bowl of chili for me – in a dog dish bowl! His three dogs were swarming territorially around me, as if they recognized the bowl belonged to one of them, and as I ate, I tried to keep from laughing at the dog with the big clown collar that kept her from licking her open wounds. It was about the least appetizing atmosphere I had ever dined in, but the chili was good! He brought out something in a test tube – it looked like soy sauce, and asked me if I wanted some of the unnamed substance, but I declined. I sat around for a few minutes after the meal, but there was nothing to talk about since we discussed issues on different levels, so I left and rode my bicycle back to my dorm in the dark, entered the bathroom and purged what little chili was still in my stomach. I could not help but feel that eating out of a dog dish bowl was what I deserved, since I was starting to deceive everyone I met.

One girl from the Ecology Club and I hit it off for awhile, but she was "too natural"; she didn't wear makeup and was very serious about not buying anything new. Now, I should have enjoyed her companionship, but once again, I felt she wasn't "my type of friend." Perhaps I was looking for a friend who was exactly like the ideal me. Maybe if I had been the "me" I wanted to be and was confident, I would have been able to accept friends who lacked some qualities I was looking for in myself. She could have taught me a lot about conservation. It did enter my consciousness that I was hurting the environment by binging and purging and that using the title environmentalist was hypocritical, but I ignored those thoughts.

Another area I explored in college was cross country running. I loved to jog, but did not know anything about competitive running and had never been to a cross country meet. As practices wore on and I jogged far behind the others, it occurred to me I was probably the worst on the team. I certainly did not feel like a runner, and running dead last at practice did not improve my social life or spirit, as I didn't talk with the team members. I quit the day of the first meet.

One final avenue of physical education I tried was teaching a fitness class for a semester. I greatly enjoyed teaching people to exercise, but the nutrition portion of the class was given to another student to teach and I resented that I could only teach exercises.

By the end of the semester I had put on eight pounds which may or may not have been noticeable to the students I was teaching, but I decided to be "honest" with them and tell them that I was a failure because I gained weight. I said I had been cheating on my diet and I was not a good role model. I'm sure the students felt like that was "a real downer!" Truly, I did feel like a failure. Fitness may have been a very good career for me had I not been a bulimic, because I liked to exercise and discovered that I received fulfillment in helping others become fit. Instead, I gave up on the idea.

Although we now know this disorder as "bulimia," I honestly did not know what was happening to me back then. The name "bulimia nervosa" was given to the disorder in 1979 and was not well-known until several years later, and the disease started for me around 1975. We also did not have the Internet, so bulimics during that time did not have easy access to information. All I knew was that I was addicted to this eating and purging process.

A food problem is a very tricky addiction to have, because food cannot be avoided. Alcohol can be kept out of the house, drugs can be kept out of the house; a person can survive quite nicely without alcohol and drugs, but everyone has to have food. Our society bonds over food, and abundant food is a primary source of entertainment and pleasure in our culture. Therefore, it cannot be avoided; it must be managed.

Most of the time I tried to ignore the binging and purging that was increasing in frequency. When I did try to confront this illness, there was no detailed battle plan, I just tried to keep busy and stay away from food. I liked crafts like knitting and crocheting, but the patterns I chose were simple and methodical, so they did not deter my mind from thinking about food. Sitting alone knitting gave me a little comfort, but at some point, I would put the needles down and go binge for awhile. Rather than take action against this oddity that was overtaking my life, I just told myself to be strong, and waited for something to change in my psyche. That wait ended up being an eleven year struggle, so simply "trying to be strong" without looking at all aspects of the problem (mental, emotional, diet misinformation), probably will not work. My weakness always upset me and it was like my brain was sabotaging itself. In truth, the only way I was strong was by fighting to keep the illness: I became very good at hiding, tricking and lying in order to get the food I wanted.

My bulimia, on good days, was once a day. There were times when binging and purging could last for most of the day. I would say I vomited anywhere from once a day up to 40 times a day. How can a person purge 40 times a day? If you count each time I drank water and threw it up to clean out my system as "one (1) vomit," the purges added up! I was so ill, yet I managed to go to school and work a few hours in addition to school, all the while jogging to "keep healthy."

With all this vomiting, one would think I didn't care about myself or my body, but the opposite is true. I sometimes ended a binge and purge session by eating something good for me, such as green beans. There were times I would eat the green beans, feel like I had eaten too many of them, and throw them up, then drink water and throw that up, drink some more and vomit more until I was sure that all of the beans were out of my system and that any bile or stomach acids were washed out too, then I would eat "the right amount of beans." Imagine my poor stomach, trying to adjust to huge quantities of food being put down; then, when my stomach sent digestive acids to match the food that was in my stomach, all of it would be vomited up, only to have more food put down, then vomited, then washed out with glass after glass of water, then more food put down! I was putting my body through terrible stress and had to be in poor health, but I thought I was doing what was best for my body by getting rid of what I ate and then eating something healthy.

Somewhere I read that a person can be addicted to the vomiting part of bulimia. Doesn't it seem as if I was a good candidate for that? I just do not know if I was addicted to purging. I believe I was not; it seems to me that I was just addicted to the desire for the taste of food, and purging was necessary after all the food that was consumed.

Vomiting and the thorough cleansing of my system could be seen as a ritual, but to me it just made sense to clean everything out and start "fresh." I needed to make sure no calories stayed in my stomach to make me fat. After awhile, it was hard to keep food down, because my "norm" was to bring it up.

It did frighten me that the singer Karen Carpenter died from heart failure due to anorexia and bulimia. I know I had to be doing some damage to my body with all the purging and worried I would get my electrolytes off-balance or have a heart attack. The only method I used with my bulimia was binging and vomiting; I did not use diuretics or diet pills because I wanted to control my weight "honestly." There is a bit of humor to my past justifications which helps offset the desire to just shake my head!

Looking into my past, my mother had a weight problem and kept detailed notebooks of her caloric intake, going back for years, and she talked about the calorie count of foods almost daily. She desired food that she couldn't have, often describing rich butter on bread or potatoes, smacking her lips, and would take a spoonful of gravy on the sly, making a guilty face. I did not want to be like that, yet my food issues turned out to be much worse!

Most women had weight problems, but it did not cause their daughters to be bulimic. My mother is not to blame for my illness. I am just noticing the guilt of food she had and I always felt sorry for her, because she would take her calories down to very low levels, with coffee and grapefruit for breakfast, year after year. I knew I did not want to eat such a small amount, always being hungry.

Eating costs money and I depended on my wonderful parents for most of it. I would call and cry that I needed a few dollars, and my tears were genuine, as strong emotions are caught up in bulimia. They would reluctantly send me some, but I did not totally mooch off of them; I worked here and there during my bulimic years, including a poor-paying 12-hour night shift from 8:00 p.m. to 8:00 a.m. at a plastic bag factory. Basically, I grabbed plastic bags off a conveyer belt and stuffed them in boxes with some twist ties and then sealed them up. Along about 2:00 a.m., I was so tired I was gluing my hand with the glue-gun instead of the box! My "go to" job was being a waitress (now called "server"), and I also worked at a pizza shop. I can hear your laughter from here: "That sounds like a brilliant place to work as a bulimic!" No pizzas were taken home, but I did eat cheese shreds in the cooler. My point is, I worked and was not totally spoiled, and appreciated the fact that I hadn't had a hard life. It was a mystery to me that I would mess up such a good life with an eating disorder and that I could not solve any of my problems.

CHAPTER FIVE

AFFECTING OTHER PEOPLE'S LIVES

At the dorms, I met a quiet girl named Phyllis who did not enjoy college life either. She was a romantic who loved poetry, and asked me to read French to her because she enjoyed the gentle sound of it. We hit it off, even though I felt she was pale, too quiet and not sporty like me. She invited me to her house in Brethren, Michigan, which was like taking a step back in time! Phyllis and I walked from her house to her grandmother's house, where Phyllis let down grandma's long, silky white hair which was "sit-upon" length, and slowly and gently brushed it. Grandma's hair looked like the fluff from milkweed, it was so soft! A stream of gentle sunlight came through the window and landed on grandma with her beautiful long tresses. It was an unforgettable moment in time.

All day in this town I saw customs so different from how I was raised. There were bearded men in hats and bib-overall blue jeans, making applesauce with a big antique-looking press. It was quite an experience and I truly enjoyed myself at Phyllis' house. We went to bed and all was well - until 3:00 a.m.

I sneaked downstairs and found a freezer. Looking inside, I saw a plastic bag with about 20 sandwiches and I consumed two of the frozen sandwiches. They seemed to be cheese with butter or mayonnaise, but I was not sure. As I ate, I wondered why so many sandwiches were in one bag. Did Phyllis' mother work for a school and I just ate two lunches meant for children? Would Phyllis' mother get fired because of me? Was she going to serve these at a party and I ate some of the food? What did I just ruin? Certainly, Phyllis' family did not have much money. Perhaps the sandwiches were for lunches for the winter. I hoped my small binge did not cause this woman too much misery. This bothers me to this day, and I am certain it will bother me for the rest of my life. The friendship between Phyllis and I dwindled away after that weekend and I do not know whether she found out about my night-time thievery, or whether we just went in different directions. I am sure I avoided her because of my guilt.

One of my most unusual experiences was living in an off-campus college apartment with three other girls. They all cooked one big meal at dinnertime and sat down together. My roommates kindly asked me if I wanted to eat with them, but I felt their meals were not healthy, as in my non-binging moments I still followed the balanced "legal" diet, which did not look appetizing to others because I did not know how to cook. I was the odd one out, and it really started to get lonely. Unfortunately, things were not going to improve. The girls discovered that food was missing, and they knew who the culprit was in the apartment. I admitted to the girls I was having a bit of a problem, but I tried to downplay it, even though I ended up crying. One of my roommates was from my high school, and it was embarrassing to have her witness my downfall. She knew me as popular and beautiful in school, but now, my image was very different. Surprisingly, instead of hating me, the girls came up with an unusual plan to help me, one that only college girls would devise!

My roommates told me they had set up a gynecological appointment for me. "Why in the world did they decide I needed to see a gynecologist?" I thought. Feeling too timid to ask, I just went to the appointment. I was a bit stunned when I walked into the room and saw a couch and chair. It turned out my appointment was not with a gynecologist, but with a psychologist! He may have been a graduate student, studying psychology, because I didn't think he was very good.

I cried a little in front of this therapist when I found out my roommates had tricked me. Then I continued to talk to him for an hour. We chatted about the usual things at first sessions: whether I was happy and if I had a good childhood. Since I had an excellent childhood, I bristled when he asked me anything about my parents. I did not want him to blame my quiet father or my educated mother for this illness of my own making. I felt like I was wasting my time and told the psychologist I was almost over this malady and would not need any help.

As I stood to leave, the psychologist gave his parting words of advice: "Barbara, have you ever made love under the stars at night?" I stood there dumbfounded, wondering where that idea came from, and said honestly, "No." He replied, "It is a beautiful experience." I awkwardly said, "Thank you," and left. This is not something a person forgets!

A month later, I was given a ride home from college by the older sister of one of my roommates. My roommate was also in the car and the older sister asked her: "What happened to that roommate you said was going crazy?" There was an awkward silence before I intervened. "That would be me. I'm fine. I'm not crazy - I'm almost cured." The awkward silence resumed. I could not wait to get out of the car.

CHAPTER SIX

CAUGHT AT CAMP

It was summer break from college and I had already decided I would not return to Central Michigan University. The campus was too large and it was too much of a party school for my taste, and the totally flat countryside was not aesthetic enough. My summer job was a welcome break and was at a camp in the beautiful Rocky mountains, so I was about to have a real adventure! A classmate from my high school, Lois, had recommended it, and we took the train out West together.

During the summer of 1976, Lois was in the cabin suite next to mine and one day she opened the door to my room without knocking. There I was with a box of crackers, a stick of Land O' Lakes butter, and some honey and jelly, and I was spreading huge globs of butter, honey and jelly onto the crackers. I made a flimsy excuse: "I like strange combinations." But a few weeks later when I was in the bathroom that joined the two rooms, I had to flush the toilet twice in order to wash all the food down that I had eaten and purged. Lois called out, "Are you all right?" With as much conviction in my voice as I could muster, I replied, "I'm just fine!" I hoped I had convinced her, and was frustrated at the inefficient toilet which should have flushed thoroughly the first time so no one would know anything was wrong.

This camp was a wonderful experience, with about 225 staff members, teens from all over the United States. For some reason, I remember a few times when we left the camp and went to restaurants. One day several of us filled a long table at a restaurant. I ordered a piece of pie, a tall sundae and a milk shake. After eating, I decided to excuse myself to use the restroom. One of the girls whose name I did not know looked directly at me and said with distain, "We know what you are going to do in there!" I was shocked, because I didn't think anyone had noticed that I had eaten more dessert than everyone else. "I'm just going to the bathroom," I said. She retorted, "Oh, right. Sure, you are!" I hesitated, but turned and went to the restroom to purge my food because I knew it would be a long time before I got back to camp, and the food would have digested. When I returned, the girl boldly asked, "Do you feel better now? We know you threw up!" Of course, I insisted, "No, I didn't. I don't do that." It was quite embarrassing, but I just stuck to myself and ignored everyone else the rest of the trip back to camp. I did not appreciate that girl making me feel guiltier than I already felt. I'm a likeable person; why did she have to notice my problem?

My only real friend in the Rockies was nature. One early morning when it was still pitch black outside, I climbed a foothill, and then sat on top to watch the sun rise over the distant mountains. It was one of the most beautiful sites I have ever seen. The clouds in the distance were outlined in iridescent pink, orange and purple, and the calm was so serene! Slowly, I watched lights at the camp come on below me, as people awakened for the day. I felt as if I owned the world and everything was perfect. Oh, what nature can do to help a person feel better! This before-dawn mountain scene, the tame deer I met on the roadway, and even the large rocks I enjoyed jumping across in the river were my comfort and my pals. Out of 225 staff members, I could only be friends with nature, because it is nonjudgmental and heals the spirit, if only temporarily.

One more dining experience comes to mind. Four of us from camp traveled to Denver to dine at a lovely, touristy Mexican restaurant, complete with young men diving into a pool and lush plants everywhere. We ate fine food, including enchiladas and chimichangas, and I especially loved the sopapillas, little pillows of fried dough with cinnamon sugar on them. Their specialty was fried ice cream and I ordered that too. When I visited the restroom after the meal, Lois, my friend from high school followed me in. I knew I would not be in a restroom again until we had returned to camp, so I devised a plan to go into the stall, bring up the food and "place" it quietly in the toilet by aiming just right so it would not hit the water and splash, and then I would turn around and sit down quickly so it would seem like I was just in there to urinate. I was skilled and felt I had been totally silent with bringing up the food as planned, but after I sat down, from the next stall Lois again called out, "Are you all right?" I guess I had spent a little too much time with my feet facing the toilet, but I said I was just fine. Could I be the only person I was fooling?

My job at camp was to mop and wax floors in a large store at night. A teen I worked with stole candy from the store and even bragged about stealing a paperback book, so I stole two candy bars and a slide of a beaver. Taking that slide of a beaver was more of a crime than taking the candy bars, because it was the first time I took something that wasn't food. From then on I worried whether the shopkeepers kept inventory of the items and knew we had stolen. That Kodachrome slide of a beaver probably cost 25 cents, and I hope I made up for it by doing a little extra work for free.

After the incident, I would hold the small slide up to a lamp to see the picture of the beaver, but I could not enjoy the slide at all, due to the guilt. Several years later, I went back to visit and spoke with the director. I told him I had worked there in 1976, and he said he remembered me. With 225 energetic teens working at camp every summer, I doubt he could possibly remember me, especially since I never talked with him before, but I worried his memories of me were of a bulimic thief. The paranoia is strong with bulimia! Years later, I threw the beaver slide away, because I could not stand to look at it and be reminded of how low I had stooped.

CHAPTER SEVEN

SOCIAL PROBLEMS ESCALATE

As autumn set in, I left Colorado and returned to Detroit to regroup and take some classes in the area. During this time I was building future memories of vomiting in my old childhood home. My beautiful sky-blue bedroom became a hiding place for small bags of vomit and vases of vomit; I would throw away the bags of vomit and wash out the vases. I suppose vomiting into bags was tidier than the sink, because the sink got clogged in the upstairs bathroom, and my dad had to come unclog it. I watched in fear as I saw bits of food in the pooled water and worried Dad would figure out I had vomited in the sink. He didn't say a word, but watching in fear, guilt and shame is a pretty good punishment. After we moved from Detroit, I had dreaded thoughts that someone buying my home would find a forgotten bag of vomit hidden in the attic off of my closet. I do think I was thorough about getting all of it out of the house, but the fear existed.

While living with my parents, they noticed how much I was crying, and they found out I had skipped some classes. After conferring with a doctor, they gave me one anti-depressant pill. A little later my mind started feeling a bit foggy. Alone in my bedroom my imagination took over. I put my hand up and looked at the shadow of my hand on the wall. It seemed to get bigger and smaller, over and over. I thought I was losing my sanity, and I panicked and screamed! My dad came upstairs and told me I was all right. He said, "You don't need any medicine." I agreed. End of discussion. We never spoke about the medicine again and I never took any more.

From reading my own words, it seems that I probably was depressed. I never thought I had any issues with depression because I hid it from myself, and denied it whenever anyone asked me if I suffered from depression. After all, I could feel as spiritual and joyful as anyone else, and I was active and in awe of nature. Throughout the bulimic ordeal, I still took long walks, jogs and bicycle rides, swam in pools and lakes, lifted weights (before it was popular for women), and tried different crafts. I wanted to be healthy! Even as a bulimic, I did not lose all my desire to have "good morals." I was vegetarian for three years – a vegetarian bulimic! My commitment was due to animals' rights, although I didn't know much about the plight of animals at that time. Certainly, it would not make sense for me to have been a vegetarian bulimic for my health! All of this does not describe a depressed person, but I now think I had a form of depression anyway.

A new malady was hindering my growth as a person, as if bulimia were not enough! I started hyperventilating, and again, I did not know what it was in the beginning. It caused me some embarrassment, as I almost passed out at college during a recital! The music recital was held at Marygrove College in Detroit, and I was supposed to sing some German aria. I did not like the song and didn't know it well, so my confidence was down. I stood in front of about eighty people, started singing, and all of a sudden became very light-headed. My arms came up and my hands met in front of me, curling into what can only be described as "severely arthritic" hands, as they cramped into a distorted pose, and I said into the microphone, "Excuse me, I think I am going to faint." Two nuns rushed up and grabbed me, one on each side, and whisked me down the aisle past all the people into the arched halls of the catholic college, where they walked me up and down the halls, with my hands slowly unfreezing from their cramped positions. From what I understand the curled up hands are caused from reduced carbon dioxide in the blood due to hyperventilation.

It gets worse. Guess who was scheduled to play a piano piece to close the recital? Yes, I was supposed to play a composition that also was too hard for me, so with my hands recently frozen in a freakish pose, I wisely declined. Thanks to me, they had no finale. Single handedly, I had ruined the entire recital! As if I did not have enough shame.

To this day I hyperventilate, since I am a person who takes on habits easily. The caffeine I drink may play a part in it, but I am not sure. I simply have learned some control techniques so that the hyperventilation does not get to the "feeling like fainting" stage, and I try to keep my caffeine within reasonable limits. I am hyperventilating right now, because if I think about it, I do it! Apparently, I still am influenced by the power of suggestion. I bet you didn't know breathing was so difficult! Managing the problem is the best "solution" for now, and since I have techniques to keep the hyperventilation mild, it is not a debilitating problem.

CHAPTER EIGHT

SEARCHING FOR MY DREAM FARMER

After living at home in Detroit, my dad and I found a small, religious college way out in the country in a beautiful farming area. It was a private school, and I hate to think what he spent for me to go there. The reason I chose Spring Arbor College was because of the scenery and to meet a dream farmer. SAC did not allow drinking, so this would be a much better college for me than CMU.

Off I went, to venture into a more protective college life at SAC, a Free Methodist affiliated school. I was not Free Methodist, and my personal beliefs vacillated between believing in my sunshiny god and doubting the existence of god. Needless to say, I felt there was a huge difference between many of the students and me, as my first roommate fretted about the devil haunting her dreams and she insisted that during the dreams, the devil was "all over the walls of our room." My suitemate had acquired a ghost named Catherine from a graveyard a few years before college, and Catherine often appeared at the edge of her bed. At least, I told myself, I was mentally more together than they were, but having my ego boosted by being a notch healthier than people with hallucinations is not much of an accomplishment. Religion was one more isolation feature for me, one more excuse not to have friends, because "they were different," and that made it easier to keep my eating disorder a secret.

One of my hidden "talents" that I discovered while at Spring Arbor College was that I could bring up select amounts of food and re-chew it, like a ruminant, and could control how much came back up. I really do not know why I did this, except that I could. Perhaps it was to make me even more unique, a specialist at bulimia, or for instant gratification. I could sit at a lunch table filled with other people, and bring up a little food and re-chew it. It seems synonymous with sucking a pacifier – a form of comfort. Sometimes I think the re-chewing also had something to do with being bored and lost. There was a dissatisfaction and impatience I had with life, even though I portrayed a person who was very calm and sure of herself on the outside.

Perhaps I am overanalyzing and simply wanted more of the same taste I had just eaten. Nevertheless, this was a horrible thing to do, because some stomach acid was most likely coming up along with the food and was wearing down my teeth. Yet food habits form quickly, and I kept re-eating my food.

When I write about odd eating disorder habits I worry that someone will try them and then I have just made someone's bulimia worse, so I warn you not to try what I did! The reason the re-chewing is mentioned here is because there may be other readers who are re-chewing their food and I want them to know that this can end.

Fig. 3

This is another old, poor-quality picture, of a picnic with my dad near a lake close to Spring Arbor College. What should have been a very fun picnic instead was filled with wondering if my dad realized I might purge what I ate as soon as I found a private place, and I loathed myself because I knew I would. I wondered whether my dad loathed me too. I look back at so many pictures from my late teens and twenties, and every nice memory is marred by the knowledge that I had bulimia at the time. There will perpetually be a cloud hanging over that eleven year period.

In my spare time, I spent hours with my old friend, nature. I would take a school book, ride my bicycle out to the country and look for my dream farmer, but the only farmers I saw were old men with missing teeth. After riding a few miles, I would stop and pull my bicycle into a cornfield, study awhile, and then fall asleep in the sun, keeping an ear out for the sound of a corn harvester. I truly enjoyed these times by myself.

Socially, I felt like a misfit, a rebel and a bad girl, because I did not attend SAC due to religious convictions. I came to find my dream farmer. One Saturday, the music director called the entire choir into the chapel. We lined up on the risers, wondering why we were having an extra practice. The director did not bring us in to sing. He said that his mother had died and he could not get over it. He told us we were like family to him, and he asked us all to pray for him. I stood there dumbfounded, thinking it was the most egotistical, selfish thing he could do! It's a beautiful day, on the weekend, and I could be out on a bicycle ride; yet here I was being asked to pray, for goodness knows how long, for someone I barely knew. Even with all his religion and faith, he could not accept the death of his mother, and wanted the strength in numbers of an entire choir praying for him. At least, that was my take on the situation. In the silence, while everyone had their heads bowed in prayer, I loudly stepped off the risers, walked all the way down the aisle of the chapel (which seemed like an endless walk), and finally out the door into the sunshine. No, I did not fit in. Perhaps a small part of me liked not fitting in, as it made me unique, but it did feel lonely.

As a personal note, I am very thankful to the powers that be at Spring Arbor College for not booting me from the college, since I also picked up a garter snake from the grass and brought it into a classroom, looking for a professor who taught us something in Bible class that I wanted to challenge, in my own way. I found him in an empty classroom, held the snake toward him and said, "All women are afraid of snakes because of Eve, hmmm?" He was quite frightened and I reveled in it, playfully taunting him and making him say, "Okay, okay, I take it back. Get the snake away from me!" Thank you, Spring Arbor College for allowing me to graduate!

While exploring the possibility of majoring in Recreation, about forty college kids went on a ski weekend in Michigan. Once again, I spent the three days making zero friends. Walking up to people and starting a conversation did not cross my mind. Unfortunately, I do not remember anything about the ski weekend (including skiing) except that someone gave me pancakes to feed to the geese on the frozen lake. I took them toward the geese, but ate a couple along the way, because everyone else was inside. Eating pancakes that were meant for the geese was very selfish of me, and I felt guilty because I knew I had to vomit them up; I needed an empty stomach for breakfast. I crept into the woods and purged in the snow and then covered it up. On my way back to the lodge, an older college student named Gary had come outside and asked me if I enjoyed feeding the geese. Something about his tone made me feel he might have witnessed me eating some of the pancakes, and I hoped he had not seen anything else! I hated feeling shame all of the time, but that is what bulimia does to a person. We reap what we sow.

After attending Spring Arbor College for a short while I started conversing with a girl who loved to talk. We chatted about boys and I described what my dream farmer would look like. One night she came over with a boy who lived on campus. He had blond hair, blue eyes and was tan, although not a chiseled farm man by any means. My friend obviously told him to put on overalls. I wanted to laugh, but I was too embarrassed by the awkward situation. He sat down on the couch and I stood across the room to keep my distance, and barely acknowledged he was there. I reasoned, "Even if I were interested, how could I get close enough to know someone with my horrible acne? Besides, I have a dark secret, so I am just not able to have a boyfriend right now." I am sure he was perplexed and felt rejected, and I am certain my friend was perturbed at me, but the fellow was not my dream farmer and I didn't want anyone meddling in my "love life."

There were very few men who caught my attention, but one whom I kept my eye on was a tall, dark, lean but strong young man at the college who was not the "momma's boy" type of guy, named Brian. He was the younger brother of Gary whom you briefly met when I talked about the geese and pancake scenario. Brian liked nature and camping, and did not seem to fit in at Spring Arbor College. He intrigued me, and I wanted to get to know him better, but I didn't see him on campus too often.

Our shower drain got plugged and my roommate called for maintenance. To my horror, who showed up at the door, but the tall, dark, handsome guy I had a crush on! Brian was about to fix the drain that I had probably plugged. I stood nearby, trying to catch a glimpse at what he was fixing, to see whether I had to make an excuse if he found many food fragments. This time, I was lucky, and he simply unclogged the drain without any "discoveries."

I think I will finish the Brian story and get him out of the picture right now. One day, he sat across the table from me in the cafeteria. He looked at me and said, "I think I am falling in love with someone; I haven't known her for long, but I can't get her out of my mind." I tried to keep a poker face, and hoped he was talking about me. He continued, "I know it is crazy, but it just seems like she's the one for me. I think I am going to ask her to marry me." Part of me was thinking it was too soon for us to get married, and part of me was thinking he was exactly my type, so it may be the fairy tale I had been looking for and wanted. Then he said, "You know her - it's Brenda." I tried to keep my face from flushing because I felt so foolish, and I was quite disappointed. Fortunately, I liked what I knew about Brenda and was happy for them, although it made me feel like no one my type would ever want to marry me.

Many times I have been thankful that I was not a drinker, because some of these disappointments surely would have driven me to drink! We have been told that if we are bulimic then we are likely to have other issues such as over-imbibing in alcohol or drugs. I cannot relate to those habits, but I did obsessively make noises when I was alone. It was a bit of a compulsive disorder, a tendency to make a funny noise a certain number of times when no one was around, and sometimes I felt I should make the noise an even number of times and sometimes it had to be an odd number of times. I developed several little compulsive behaviors that had to do with doing a movement a certain number of times. These groundless habits lasted for a few years, but totally left me when I no longer believed any kind of superstitious ritual would bring me luck or keep me from having bad luck.

Now that I think about it, I did have some issues other than the eating disorder. I had been having an exaggerated fear of even the slightest heights such as driving over a viaduct. This trepidation never disappeared, but I can handle viaducts now and at least a fear of heights is common!

One day, around 1978, while shopping, I had trouble breathing and felt lightheaded. My heart seemed like it had sped up and I was afraid I was having a serious heart issue. I drove to the nearest hospital in Jackson, Michigan, walked in the emergency room and politely stated, "I think I am having a heart attack." They hooked me up to an EKG, checked me out thoroughly, and told me I was having a panic attack and was hyperventilating. With a "clean bill of health" I left the hospital, feeling foolish that my breathing and anxiety issues had tricked me into thinking I was going to die. I wonder if the bulimia had anything to do with the panic attack, or whether it was due to caffeine, or some other reason.

As the semesters ticked away at Spring Arbor College, I had more new roommates. Switching living quarters was about the only constant in my life, besides bulimia! My excuse to change roommates was that the girls were not my type, but perhaps I felt I had to move on because of my secret. This time I roomed with some very nice girls, but I risked the friendliness we had built up by using some of a roommate's homemade powdered milk (I am assuming it was from a cow). My roommate noticed right away and talked with the other roommate about how someone had been stealing her milk, and I overheard them. I quickly made up an excuse why I had to use it, and they whispered quietly to each other, "Can you believe it? She took it! Oh my gosh!" I had betrayed girls whom I truly liked and I know they could have been my friends, but I was ill. That's all there is to it.

Attending class regularly during these years was difficult, but not because of the bulimia. Sometimes my acne was so bad I did not want to be seen, so I skipped classes. The next two paragraphs will sound "repulsive" but I want to prove how bad my skin actually was most of the time. I used to have scabs on several areas of my face because the pimples had been so deep that they formed scabs once I thoroughly removed their contents. Since I did not want to go to class with scabs on my face, I would take a pair of scissors and carefully cut the surface scabs off, then wash, then get it as dry as possible, take foundation and cover the raw area and then put powder on it and go to class with a smooth-looking outer layer on my face. Just some minor surgery before class! I took backup foundation and powder for touch ups, because these wounds sometimes leaked liquid. The smooth look only lasted a few hours, because the scabs reformed. There were times I could not get the bleeding to stop, or my face would be swollen, and on those days I would skip classes.

It is difficult to boost self-esteem when the body works against itself. One last anecdote must be told about acne. I spent a summer on staff at a camp in Petoskey, where I was outside most of every day, sometimes in the woods, and other times lying on the docks in the sun, getting tan. There I was, baking my skin with my horrible acne, and my skin started itching and swelling. No one knew what was wrong with my skin, but the director of the camp insisted that I go to a doctor to make sure I was not contagious.

The doctor said he was not sure what was wrong either, and took a slide sample, but never found any bugs under my skin. Still, he decided I had scabies and prescribed Kwell lotion. This is another potent lotion that should not be put on the skin more than once due to side effects such as dizziness and possible seizures, but I applied it several times, because the itching continued and I thought the bugs under my skin just would not die. It was so demeaning and gross and I felt so dirty. I could not understand why bugs would decide to camp out under my skin. My cousin was the only person who looked at me and said, "As a teacher, I have seen cases of scabies and you do not have scabies." Everyone else joked and called out to me, "Hi Barb! How are your pets?" Yes, it is funny, but it hurt at the time.

Since those days at camp many years ago, I have been bitten by sand fleas or what is called "no-see-ums" many times. A lot of the spots look just like the bites I remember and the itching is the same, so I think no-see-ums were a part of the problem. Also, it dawned on me that I started itching after every shower I took, as well as being in the sunshine, and discovered I am one of the rare people allergic to heat! With my cystic acne, hives and no-see-um bites combined, I was misdiagnosed and had to wear long sleeves for a few weeks in the summer. The mental anguish and embarrassment were worse than the itching! This was another time I was happy to leave a camp and return to college.

It is a wonder I did fairly well in college, but most of my "success" was because I dropped several classes and switched to courses that were easier for me. I was determined to graduate but was not wise enough to see how my decisions affected my future, and never knew much about the importance of seeking a financially sound career. Perhaps a good counselor could have helped me. I seemed to need a counselor in several areas of my life!

In case the totality of colleges I attended is confusing, I went to more than I have mentioned. The total number of colleges is eight. Sometimes I would attend three colleges at the same time, i.e., (U of M Dearborn, Henry Ford Community College and Marygrove College) and later (Jackson Community College, Albion College and Spring Arbor College). All credits, along with the credits from my first two years at Central Michigan University were transferred to Spring Arbor College so I could graduate. (Later, I attended North Central Michigan College.) The most I can say in my defense is that my finagling of classes and colleges showed some determination.

After all these years of college, student teaching was the last semester. My plan was to graduate with an Education degree, Music major and French minor. I settled on Music for my major, because even though my voice was nothing like it had been pre-tonsillectomy, music was the subject I knew the best and it became my default career, since nothing else panned out, and the required courses did not involve math.

I began student teaching with high hopes, but I only lasted a week! It felt like I was just one step ahead of the high school kids when teaching French and it did not feel natural standing in front of kids with a baton, waving my arms in Music class. Going to a religious college did not prepare me with a repertoire of songs for public schools, I lacked confidence, and these subjects were just not right for me to teach.

After six and a half years of college, I dropped my teacher's certificate and just graduated with a Liberal Arts degree, and there was nothing I could do with my meager skills in music and French. My graduation cord and certificate were shipped out to Colorado at Keystone Ski Resort where I took a job "butt-bucketing" (picking up trash and cigarette butts with a little broom and dust bin) and I wore my gold cord as I butt-bucketed around the resort. I thought it was funny, but I should have taken my education more seriously. Certainly my parents were not pleased, but my mother said that she was not surprised. I was adamant that I did the right thing by dropping the student teaching. The high school students seemed bored with life, and they had no interest in me. I thought I would be the cool teacher everyone loved. Instead, I was watching them live their sleepy lives, but I was not a part of the mix. This is why I returned to the mountains to work at a ski resort in the summertime, with no goals beyond that, and I brought my same old problems along for the ride.

CHAPTER NINE

ONE EMBARRASSING SITUATION AFTER ANOTHER

Colorado was a welcome retreat after the academic years. I found an apartment near Keystone and moved in with another girl named Cathy. She was not at the apartment much, and I started eating a little of her cereal, some butter, some milk and used her salad dressing on my salad. I tried to cover my tracks as much as I could, taking the one half stick of butter that was left and putting it back with the closed end flush with the three complete sticks, so that it would look like there were four complete sticks to the pack, and adding some water to the milk and the salad dressing to bring the levels up. She noticed every single bit of the food that was missing, and knew I added water to the milk and salad dressing! It's almost as if a camera were hidden in the apartment, so observant was she of food that was missing. Cathy was one person who was direct with me, and it frightened me because I did not want to change. I felt I could not change, so I moved out.

There was one more incident that was just shameful that occurred in Colorado. I had driven down to Denver, and after eating various foods including pink ice cream, I stopped at a gas station that had a bathroom on the outside with a key to unlock it. When I unlocked the restroom, the toilet bowl was already plugged. I still went in and purged the food that was in my stomach, so the plugged toilet looked like it was topped with pink ice cream. As I opened the door, I was mortified to see a woman and her young son who wanted to use the facilities. I handed her the key and left as quickly as possible, and broke into a run as they went into the restroom. I knew she and her son would see that ice cream topped toilet and I did not want to be nearby. I ran for three blocks and then stayed away, worrying all the while what she would have to tell her son and whether they would be shocked and sickened. After I was certain they were gone from the area, I circled around and got into my car. When I think about this scene, it still horrifies and disgusts me. I feel so sorry for what I did.

A few weeks later, I met a man who was positive, funny and charming. I will not say much more about him, because I do not want to delve into the relationship. But we ended up getting married. I thought my dream had come true, and in many ways, it had; there were dreamy moments and wonderful experiences. However, he and I had some issues, with both of us bringing problems we could not help into the mix.

My acne had a little to do with our relationship and my confidence. I really did try everything possible for my skin. I used prescription tetracycline for years, and when I could not afford the prescription, I purchased tetracycline from a pet store, because tetracycline was used in the aquariums. Do not do this, because not only is it hard to know how much you are taking, but also whether it is just tetracycline, since it is only supposed to be a low grade medicine for tropical fish. Also, in hindsight, I think it may not be legal, but someone at a pet store told me he used the tetracycline that went into the fish tanks, so I did it a few times too. When my husband at the time and I moved to a small town in Oregon where there were no pet stores, I went to a feed store to purchase some tetracycline, and stood with the owner of the store looking at labels. We figured I was bigger than a chicken and smaller than a cow, so a large spoonful of the tetracycline powder mixed with water should be the right amount for a human. Mixing it with water looked and tasted a lot like a bitter Metamucil. Oh, the foolish things I did! Unfortunately, it did not do much to improve my skin.

My bulimia was not severe during my marriage, relatively speaking, but I do remember waking up a few times to eat at night. We had a drifter named Kenny staying with us for awhile who slept on the floor. A couple of times I sneaked out of bed and stepped over Kenny to get to the kitchen to eat. Hopefully, he slept through my nighttime thievery! As far as I know, I hid these problems from my husband. Judging by all the other times I thought I was secretive enough, there is a possibility he knew, but never confronted me, as we were kind to each other.

Opportunities were few in a very small town on the coast of Oregon, so we packed up and moved to Idaho and then Washington. Kenny stayed behind and we lost contact with him, but he was a nice fellow and we knew he would be all right. A few rentals and a few jobs later my spouse and I made a mutual decision.

CHAPTER TEN

STARTING OVER AGAIN

We ended our marriage. After two and a half years, I packed up what I could fit in my small car and drove across the country from Spokane, Washington to Roscommon, Michigan where my parents had moved from Detroit. The trip back to Michigan was exhausting, both physically and emotionally. I cried in the car, at rest stops, and at a restaurant in a dinky town where a young couple was making out. My dreams had been shattered, and before I went to bed, I took off my wedding ring in a little motel room in the middle of nowhere, Wyoming, and cried some more.

By this time, I was 27 years of age. I always enjoyed spending time with my parents, but I still had not conquered my problems, so I was probably more grateful to be with them than they were to have me home again. I threw up after most meals, lying to my parents all the time, and my mother finally confronted me. She said she would pay for me to be in the hospital. I insisted I did not want to go, and would handle the illness myself. Truly, I was afraid if I entered a hospital, they would not let me out! I pictured it with gray walls and I would be wearing a hospital gown and have stringy hair, and more frightening than that was that doctors would decide what I would eat. Perhaps if I had imagined spaghetti and cookies, I might have been more willing to be admitted to the hospital, but I didn't - I imagined hospital food at its worst! I was also afraid I would be forced to be with other people I didn't like and my desire to live would disappear. More than anything, I did not want to stop my life, even though I had nothing and no goals. The hospital was out!

By this point, my mother was getting bolder, and she also was sick of seeing me waste my life. She flashed some money in front of my face and said, "Why don't I just flush this down the toilet, because that's where it will end up!" Yet, I kept up my bulimic routine, and she had to cash a T-bill that had been saved for my parents' comfort in their older years. When reading about me, it seems like I was a thoughtless, selfish, shallow, spoiled young woman, and perhaps I was, but I really did a lot of "soul searching" and tried to figure out how to change my ways. As most bulimics do, I sincerely thought I was trapped and helpless in my illness. I also felt quite bad that my parents were upset, because I was the reason my dad would fuss about expenses and my mom would be visibly worried about me. I had shattered their perfect world too.

In order to get me moving in a positive direction again, my mother took me to a dermatologist and they put me on Accutane for the fourth time. It greatly helped rid me of the worst of the cystic acne and cleared up my chest, back, arms and legs. My face still had acne, but at least it improved. My mother then offered one more kind gesture - to send me back to college, if I could find a career I truly wanted to achieve.

Looking at my possible career choices, there was always a reason not to choose any of them. I finally told her I wanted to become a word processor, because I could work as any kind of secretary or live anywhere and find a job. My mother was disappointed in that "low career bar," as she had worked her way through college, earning a Bachelor's degree in Education with a double masters in Zoology and English and a double minor in Biology and Journalism (the order may be wrong, but the subjects are right – I never could keep straight what all she had accomplished)! Still, she let me enroll at North Central Michigan College in Petoskey, Michigan. It was a less expensive college, so I did not feel too bad about going back to school on her dime.

At North Central I enrolled in word processing classes, but had trouble figuring out the computer. This was the first time I had ever used one. The cursor was "jumping all over the screen" as I could not catch on to the mouse/cursor relationship! The other members of the class either had no problem learning how to use the computer, or did not let on they were confused, because I felt like the sole idiot in the room. I quickly dropped those classes but did not tell my parents. To make it look like I was still enrolled in the secretarial classes, I took out a book from the library on speedwriting to learn enough to fake like I was doing homework if I went home for the weekend. I also taught myself foreign languages (enough to ask for food and a bathroom), convinced it would help me in life.

There was one suitemate in college in whom I confided, and she stuck by my side and was a loyal friend, although we did not do much together. She fussed at me and told me I should get off my behind and go to some classes, but then I showed her that I could speak a little Spanish, Italian and German besides the bit of French I already knew, and she was impressed and decided I knew what I was doing!

Since my new career choice wasn't working out at college, I made a decision to become an entertainer. I could still sing decently if I didn't break out in tears, and all I needed was an instrument. A guitar has too thick a neck for my taste, so I decided on the banjo. I would be a singing banjo player! I imagined myself in front of a maroon curtain with a spotlight shining on me as I entertained crowds, so I bought a $200 banjo and took a few lessons. I proudly showed my mom my purchase. My mother "hit the roof" and I remember her using the expression, "That is the last straw!" She scolded me for wasting both my money and hers. I tried to explain it was going to be my new career and that it was a wise purchase, but she just did not understand!

I was upset that she called me out on my poor purchase, but part of me knew I should not have spent the money. Playing the banjo was much harder than I thought, so I sold it to the man who had given me the lessons.

Back at the dorm, I still took occasional trips to the grocery store. I made a list of what I needed and told myself this time I would just get what is on the list. It started out fine, but less than a minute inside of the store, I felt a crazy urge come over me. My hands would even sweat! I was driven to buy candy bars, cookies, donuts, cheese, just about anything fattening. This must have been some strange reaction to anxiety; a way of not worrying about anything else, a way of getting everything I wanted, a way to have a moment of passion, and a way to have something constant that I could count on in my life. After returning to the dorm, partaking in the big binge and the necessary purge, the usual remorse set in.

With so many years of failing myself, I decided to try one more counselor. Walking into the room, I was met by a small, meek woman who looked quite young. Instantly, I felt I could tell her what to do. She spent the hour asking me about my childhood and I was a bit offended. Why do psychologists always think childhood is the problem? She asked me some other questions and I had a "brilliant" answer for everything, and felt I had shown her I did not need counseling services. At the end of the hour, she asked, "What day can you come back next week?"

I felt my mouth drop open. "Next week? What will I do until then?" She did not say anything in response, and it entered my mind that I would binge as soon as I got back to my room, to prove that the session was not worth my time. Frankly, I worried about what the next week would bring. I might die! I told her I would call her, and left for good. She had not solved my problem; she hadn't improved me at all!

As you can see, I did not understand that there was more than one problem caught in this bulimic web and that I needed to talk with a counselor until my defenses came down and we could start exploring the causes. I have read that the most common way to treat bulimia is with cognitive behavioral therapy on an out-patient basis. Had I stuck with the therapy, I may have ended the binging sooner. Perhaps I needed a different counselor than the two I tried. Maybe I would have had more success with a "life coach"; a constant cheerleader who would shout, "You can do it!" Yet, chances are I would have made that person my enemy too; someone to lie to, someone to disappoint.

It is so unfortunate that I went to the therapist to get help and then spent my time there trying to prove I did not need help! The only person I convinced was me. It was pointless to go to therapists if I was going to work against them and myself. I do not blame the counselors, and I would blame myself for giving up so easily, but I was in over my head with this psychiatric disorder.

CHAPTER ELEVEN

THE MINISTER IS UNCOMFORTABLE

Most people would not admit what I am about to share with you. The reason I am divulging this information is because I want to show you how impulse can rob all sense of dignity, and take us down to levels we never imagined. There were about four "lowest points" in my bulimia days that readily come to mind. This one is definitely the grossest! I was alone in my room at college, eating chocolate ice cream, and after consuming quite a bit of the container I purged the chocolate ice cream into a sink. Before rinsing it down the drain, I realized since I had just eaten the ice cream and immediately brought it back up it would still be edible, so I taunted myself to eat some, and after pausing to think about it, I ate five bites. I purged that too, because no ice cream, re-eaten or fresh could stay in my system!

I think, subconsciously I had to re-eat it because it was the most deplorable thing I could think of to do, or possibly because the urge that teased me was impossible to resist once I thought of it. I was strong-minded about staying away from alcohol and drugs and had no urges, yet so weak when it came to food impulsiveness. Did my subconscious mind cause my desire for the ice cream in the sink because I wanted to "hit rock bottom?" Did I want to feel bad about myself or did I think it was cool being that bad? I do not know. It is so demeaning that maybe I felt I deserved to be that disgusting.

We are conditioned to think we must be at our lowest point before we can recuperate, but that is not true. We could turn ourselves around at any time. I hit rock bottom with this "ice cream in the sink" scenario, and I wish I could say it was my turn-around point, but it was not.

As I was driving one day, I was feeling quite blue. I thought about all of the organizations that had failed me and I did not know what to try next. When I saw a church on the right, I stopped and went up the steps. The door was not locked so I entered and started looking around for something on the walls that would help me, as I had an idea of what I needed. A minister found me wandering the halls, and directed me into his office. I told him about my eating disorder and that I just needed something to make me stop. I asked him if he had any pictures of starving children in Africa on the walls, or anything to make me feel really guilty. The minister seemed taken aback and did not know what to say. I think he may have been shocked about the eating disorder and perhaps was a bit grossed out by me. The visit was very awkward, and he offered no pictures of starving children for me to see. I do not remember his advice, but I do remember that it was unremarkable and left me feeling empty.

My newest "home" was in a boarding house in Petoskey, Michigan. There were about ten people, each renting a room, along with one cupboard per person in the kitchen. The first thing I noticed was that the renters kept food in their cupboards but they rarely cooked. There were quick items in the cupboards and I started sneaking a little jelly, a piece of bread, a cookie, a few chips; food I thought would no one would miss. The boarders were gone all day, which made taking food easy. After awhile, someone mentioned there might be a food thief, but no one seemed to think it was sweet Barbara. Between bouts of despair, the usual thought was that I would be able to lick this illness any day. Meanwhile, with ten people living at the boarding house, it was only a matter of time before someone would take a day off and "catch me in the act," so I moved out.

After the boarding house, I lived for a very brief while with another bulimic. We thought the arrangement would be perfect because we could help each other, but she was one of those "occasional bulimics," who overate and purged due to a direct emotional stimulation, such as breaking up with a boyfriend, losing a job or failing a test. We said we would have each others' backs, but we were very different and she was off working and socializing. She looked like a success to me, and I felt even more despair and loneliness. I was working only a few hours a week and had too much time on my hands, and I spent most of it binging and purging.

While shopping for myself at the local grocery store, the cashier asked me if I owned a bakery. I guess I bought staples like butter and sugar a little too often! I did not want a stranger knowing my problem, so I told the cashier I loved to bake and throw parties. Nothing was going my way. I fell into a deep pit at this apartment, mixing dried milk and sugar with a bit of water – anything I could find. I felt betrayed that my roommate was so healthy and didn't seem to care that I was not doing well. She probably thought I was too different from her, just as I thought she was too different from me. We weren't friends, so I made arrangements to move out and she had been doing the same.

There was a very attractive and friendly girl who lived in the Petoskey area who seemed as if she could be a true friend of mine. She was so easy going and loved to converse. She was one of those lucky girls, with beautiful skin and her boyfriend was the grandson of an owner of a world-renowned toy company. I felt cool just being around her. When I visited her house she told me about some of the interesting things she did, such as working as a hand model. I went into her bathroom and in the cabinet I found a bottle of chewable Vitamin C. It tasted so good I ate at least ten, quickly purging them. I always wanted to go back to her house so I could have some more Vitamin C, but I never saw her again.

It does bother me now that I have written about all the times I stole other people's food and that the totality is much more than I realized. It seems as if my morals disappeared; I certainly was not making use of them! I think they were always there, but they took a back seat to emotional needs. If there are other bulimics reading this who take other people's food, I want to assure you that once you are over this illness, if you are like me, you will revert to your earlier morals of "never even thinking about taking someone else's food." I never steal anything. It's kind of fascinating to see how our morals are malleable by our mental condition.

Occasionally, I talked with my parents on the phone and in one of the conversations my mother mentioned she was enrolled in a new diet group and that the meetings were fun. I decided to go to the local chapter in my town, because I figured a professional organization might be able to help me. I was greatly mistaken. Looking at my small frame, the head of the group asked why I was there. I said I had about five pounds to lose and that I had bulimia, but wanted to lose weight the right way, and I thought some support would help. The look she gave me, the tone of her voice, and the silence from the rest of the group let me know I was not welcome. I had just embarrassed myself, made them angry and they were insulted by my presence. They told me at the end of the meeting they did not think their group was right for me, and I agreed.

CHAPTER TWELVE

GIVING HYPNOSIS A WHIRL

After leaving North Central Michigan College and the Petoskey area, I went downstate to find a job, staying at my brother's house for a short while in a lovely small town. He graduated college several years before I did, married, had kids, and became successful from the start. I was embarrassed he had to have me as a sister. Of course, I took food out of his cupboards too. His wife bought carob chips and made granola of which I selfishly ate huge amounts. I always awakened in the middle of the night to binge. After one such binge, I heard my sister-in-law and brother talking in their bed. Their voices were soft, but it sounded like they were talking about me. I felt horrible that I was disturbing their lives and silently cried, knowing I was not strong enough to pull myself out of this hole that was my weary existence.

I begged God to stop me, and prayed for help. My sobs were gut-wrenching and I pleaded for an end to the bulimia. Unfortunately, the binging continued. I would scold myself, saying in my head: "Get a grip, grow up!" It was even more frustrating to think I was trying so hard, at my wit's end, and there was no change in my behavior. I just wanted to be the old me.

I still toss around ideas of why I woke up at night. Was it a fear of being without food for so many hours? Did my brain just go haywire? Today I am still not certain. Perhaps there were several reasons that reinforced each other. It recently came to me that getting up at night felt sneaky, and it was a way to have the place to myself. There was peacefulness to the nighttime quiet. Eating at that time was more like fantasy than reality. I did not feel as accountable, because waking up at 3:00 was "something I could not help" since it was in the middle of the night and I was "half-asleep" so I did not have full control. Perhaps I also woke up at 3:00 a.m. so that I could do what I wanted, without anyone being around to tell me otherwise. It could have been symbolic for wanting to make my own choices. That is sad in itself, since the choice I was making was such a deceitful one.

In desperation to find out why I kept waking up in the middle of the night to binge, I went to a hypnotist. He was a nice man who gave me some preliminary tests and proclaimed I hypnotized quite easily. He talked me into a light hypnotic, relaxed state, then, after I had been hypnotized awhile, he asked, "Why do you wake up at 3:00 a.m.?" There was supposed to be a huge revelation, but my mind was a total blank. Nothing! There was no answer, no reason! I instantly came out of the light trance and started crying. This was another dead end, and I was devastated. How was I going to solve "No reason?"

It always discourages me to see how easily I gave in to impulses and urges – there was not much of a determined fight for all the "pondering" I did over the years. I have to stress that bulimics try to stop all the time and just do not have the mind-frame to take control. I argued with myself almost every day. Sometimes it was a short fight, where I simply put off trying until another day: "Tomorrow I will eat right." But many times, I would agonize over how awful I was, and search my brain to figure out how to change. Some of my long walks in nature were not that enjoyable because I spent all that time arguing with myself. Although I anguished about my problems, I never created a detailed plan to get rid of the bulimia.

Living alone created easier opportunities for binging, and it could be frightening. Many times I was consumed by hours of binging and purging and I wondered if it would ever end - as if I were an object taken over by the illness, with no choices. With bulimia, there is no set stopping point. Since fullness does not matter, bulimics are at the mercy of their energy levels, their desires, and the amount of good food; and each bulimic eventually decides when a binge is over, often with no conscious reasoning.

Binging could become dangerous. Sometimes when I vomited, I did feel a bit dizzy, and one time I scratched my throat on one of those tiny grains from

Grape Nuts cereal. I remember lying down by the toilet once because I was just exhausted and afraid I was dying, but I am sure I was nowhere near death. I proclaimed, "Never again! This was the last time!" We know how long those intentions lasted – right up to the next temptation.

I could be sitting, very contently, watching television, and the urge to binge would come out of nowhere. There was very little fight from me, and I truly felt there was no way to change course. Before I knew it, I was scouring the refrigerator to see what combinations I could put together, even if it was a peanut butter, butter, honey, jelly, potato chip and banana sandwich with more chips on the side.

When driving in town, my attention was on the restaurants I was passing and the plans I was making to check out their food. It was not unusual to stop at three restaurants and order "to go" foods, so I could eat the food at home. Not once did I change my mind or stop a binge of my own accord.

What I notice about therapists, friends, and relatives – they all became problems to me when I had bulimia. If they were trying to help me, I had to be trickier in binging. I had to outsmart them. Then, I had to avoid them. Was it that I did not want them to control me? Did it have to do with personal freedom? Or was I just too ashamed that I needed help? If you find you are thinking about your family and friends as if they are nuisances, getting in the way of your food, realize this is a part of your mind that has been poisoned by bulimia. I was not as afraid that they would keep me from eating as I feared that I would eat thousands of calories and right then the doorbell would ring and a friend would keep me from being able to rid my stomach of the food! How many pounds would I gain? What would happen to my body with all that fatty food going through it? This is a huge reason friendships did not last or were not formed in the first place.

Eating normally is very difficult for some of us, because we want to be able to control all of our food choices, with portions that are just right so our weight will be perfect. But eating as a healthy person is not like that at all! At some meals normal people eat a little too much and at others they just tide themselves over with a snack. Normal eaters still have to control their food intake to some extent, but it is not a rigid control. The unknown is always there, and that is a hard concept for many bulimics.

CHAPTER THIRTEEN

HELP FROM AN UNLIKELY SOURCE

Just when it seemed like there was no solution for my disorder, I found a group that gave me a little power over my "gluttonous self" and I only attended the meeting once, but was given an invaluable management skill to help with the problem of waking up at 3:00 a.m. to eat. This was a group I knew nothing about, but part of the title of the group was "Willpower." Developing willpower had to be helpful!

Much of the meeting was not useful to me. There were people at the meeting with whom I could not relate because they were struggling with mental illnesses, and I was not comfortable being around people who needed personal help to stay sane. The organization seemed to have some type of "step" program, but the only part I clearly remember was the idea to command the muscles not to move. They said to repeat commands to oneself, such as, "I will not wake up at 3:00 a.m., I will not wake up at 3:00 a.m.," or "I will not move, I will not move." They claimed that the muscles follow the commands of the brain. I tried this, repeating the statements many times during the day and before I went to bed. Lo and behold, it worked! I did not wake up at 3:00 a.m.! I repeated the commands for several days, and never again did I awaken at 3:00 a.m. to eat. I know this sounds unbelievable and too ridiculously easy, but for me, this was the answer to that specific problem. It seemed to break the habit. Had I been wise, I would have expanded this willpower technique to command my body not to buy sweets, not to go into a restaurant, not to binge and purge! But it never once crossed my mind.

I did not go back to the Willpower group, because one of the men with a mental illness was quite talkative and needy, and little attention was paid to me. I also did not care for the idea that I was worthless and helpless without a higher power. I had already tried the higher power idea many times, and I really wanted my own power. I did not want be told I was weak; that is what I was trying to solve! I wanted to feel worthy as a person, and I wanted to solve this with my own strength. A step-based program is fine for the majority of people; it just was not right for me.

Battling the problem with a full effort would have shown strength, but we know I did not try that hard. From my experiences, I can make some recommendations about what might work for you. Don't wait until the next meal, the next day, because this was a common excuse for me: "Tomorrow I will not binge . . . this will be the last time." My thoughts about how to take control are to make a plan for the next moment - how you will refrain from binging when you are in your house by yourself. Look up some groups in your area, and see if one seems like a good fit. You might need to shop around to find a group with whom you relate and mesh well, or you need to accept that you might not like everyone in the group!

One problem with a group meeting is that you may not get a chance to speak. Some people tend to monopolize the talking time, unless you have a strong and fair leader. I had problems with group therapy because I did not want bulimic friends or former bulimic friends, and I did not want to talk about the subject because I wanted to live a life free from the subject of bulimia! I also did not want to hear how well other people were doing. Another thing my mother told me is that I tend to have a negative, critical attitude.

Instead of how I behaved, try to learn from other people's experiences, feel sorry for them and not just yourself. Realize you won't be in the group forever, but for now, it is necessary. In the long run, trying from a determined standpoint is better than giving half your effort or not trying at all.

There were other people in an overeating therapy group I attended only one time, who talked openly about their problems with food. I remember a young woman who claimed her bulimia was under control, but I wondered if she really had it licked. She seemed a bit narrow-minded about her advice. Sugar was always the root of her evil; she said she was totally addicted to sugar and had to stay away from it at all costs. She proudly told the group that she had to read a book at every meal as a distraction from the food so she would not pay attention to the taste, and always had a salad for dinner. I could not see this as a long-term cure, and did not want to be fearful of all foods except salad and then read a book to keep me from tasting the salad. I wanted to learn to enjoy food in good amounts.

I had already gone through stages where I had "safe foods" and salad was one of them. Staying away from certain foods and calling them evil (or illegal) was the way my illness began to show itself years ago! Identifying as an addict and never allowing even a smidgen might work for alcoholics, but food is everywhere, so I would rather learn to manage it than be afraid of it. After all, this young woman had not gotten rid of the problem; she was just avoiding it. Yet, this girl with the salads and book seemed so sure of herself, that it just made me feel worse.

For all of the talk about how empty I felt, my life was not that difficult. There are a lot of people in the world with much worse problems than mine, and they do not engage in binge-purge sessions. At least, in my case, the bulimia must have had to do with coping ability. Two of my issues with coping were my fear of criticism and of being disliked. These are probably difficult issues for everyone. What I have learned is if you put forth the effort to like someone and in return are given snide remarks, then it should not hurt to be disliked by them. After all, you know you did your part, and they have made a decision to be unfriendly. Don't satisfy them by feeing hurt.

Attractive people who are not nice cease to be attractive. That is something I learned with the 12-hour night factory job. There were four lines at the factory we could work on and two of us were on each line, working together. Every two hours, we rotated machines and had new partners for the next two hours. A new employee started working there, a very pretty young woman. Each guy who talked to me when they were on my line, said they couldn't wait to meet the new girl and work with her. I have to admit, I felt a little jealous. Each guy spent two hours on the same line where she was working, and when each returned to me, they said they were so thankful to be back working with me! Apparently, the girl did not talk much, seemed standoffish and was "dumb as a rock." I felt a bit sorry for her because not everyone gets the opportunity for a good education, but the fact that she was not pleasant certainly made her much less appealing to young men who were as bored as I was with putting plastic bags in boxes! I must admit, it did make me feel better that my co-workers enjoyed spending their two hours talking with me.

There are many helpful tips to try in order to help your mood. Our world is so complex and stressful that I feel a little meditation can be beneficial, and it is not something I tried until recently. Slowing down a bit and de-stressing has been shown to have health benefits. Because of my hyperventilation habit, I cannot "pay attention to my breathing," but I have found a different form of meditation that helps. We know that if the mind is too quiet, meditation might backfire due to boredom and images of food might flood the head. However, thoughts can be guided, such as, "I am a strong person" or other empowering words, so that the mind will not veer off course.

Try any form of meditation that makes you feel better, such as relaxing, visualizing beautiful scenery, or listening to the quiet. I personally do not want to meditate for fifteen minutes, because it is not my style and would feel like I was being punished for eternity. My quickie method (when I remember to do it) is to sit and relax my muscles and then repeat words in my head, such as, "enjoy, happy, smile." My meditations last a maximum of one minute, but they still help calm my nerves! If you think about words that make the corners of your mouth turn up, it helps greatly with stress.

At work, I use another method to de-stress. I keep a bird book at my desk, and twice a day, I read a short paragraph on a bird. Not only do I learn more about birds, but getting my mind off of work issues for a second and reading something interesting helps take down my stress level. Plus, there always is a pretty picture of a bird on the page to brighten my day! My "meditations" may be unorthodox, but they work for me, and I am sure you can find a form of meditation you like and mold it to your lifestyle.

CHAPTER FOURTEEN

THE UNIMPRESSIVE CURE

I wish I could solve bulimia for everyone with a one-step, simple plan! Unfortunately, the way I became well is not anything like that. How did I cure my bulimia? Be prepared to be underwhelmed! I moved from my brother's house to an apartment in Troy, Michigan and had been working as a receptionist at a law firm. Even though I did not find the subject of law inspiring, I enjoyed the position as receptionist, talking with people on the phone, greeting everyone who came in the door and occasionally typing legal documents for attorneys. I was praised by the office manager and others in the office for my abilities and most of the staff seemed to like me. It appeared that I was finally on a career path I could handle and I felt hopeful.

My face was still speckled with acne and I even mentioned it in the interview when the office manager was trying to decide whether or not to hire me. I had some scabs across my nose but told him, "My acne is not usually this bad," because I was afraid he would not hire me for a receptionist position since I had to greet people. Thankfully, he hired me anyway!

I still binged and purged, but it was less often and less drastic. In my spare time, I was dating and found a person who was trustworthy, with a good job and a lot of nice relatives, and it seemed like the lifestyle I wanted, so this area of my life was improving too. He was older and seemed secure, and I think subconsciously I felt I would not have to worry about much in life with him, because he was mature and already had lived on his own for years. He offered security and steadiness, which had been missing for years from my life. He flew up to see me from Atlanta, Georgia, because he worked for the airlines and could fly for free. That still took some dedication, as he had to rent a car and a hotel on weekends in order to visit. I knew I had to make a decision, as long distance relationships are expensive.

My last binge-purge session was in early April, 1987. A combination of events all at once stopped the bulimia, and you have already read some of the reasons! First, I was receiving praise on the job, enjoyed participating at work, and felt more content. Second, the Willpower method of refusing to get up and eat at night - simply refusing to move my muscles gave me a victory and a little hope. Third, I burned out on bulimia. This is probably the most important number, and the one I cannot teach. I simply was tired of being bulimic and I did not want to vomit anymore. Instant gratification by gorging was no longer very satisfying. The desire not to do it became stronger than the desire to do it. Fourth, I married a second time. Planning a wedding helped keep me occupied with other thoughts. Fifth, my husband-to-be was with me as often as possible and we participated in social activities. Sixth, immediately after we were married we went on our honeymoon, and then directly moved to Atlanta, Georgia. This was enough to totally break the binge/purge habit that had been waning for awhile.

It may have been the day before the wedding or the day of the wedding that was my last extra bowl of cereal, still bringing portions back up to re-chew before I purged it. I honestly cannot remember "the last meal." All I know is that I found myself eating normally with no problem at the wedding, and thereafter. Now, do not misunderstand, I am not recommending that anyone go out and get married to end their bulimia! Remember, I was married once before and it did not cure me. My bulimia ended from the culmination of being ready to quit bulimia and move on, along with having more confidence, getting involved in social activities, and taking a break from my own food. As I said, I cannot give you an exact magic formula that will work for you, but I think you can examine your own life and see where you can help yourself. If you can improve two or three areas, and find a way to get away from having easy access to food or perhaps have some planned meals and nothing else available for a few days, it may be enough to change course!

What surprised me was that I went from being a food junkie to normal with no effort at all, after all those years of struggle and fear. Perhaps I forgot to be afraid of food because I was too busy living. It is embarrassing to say I was 30 years of age, but I was finally free from bulimia! Admittedly, it is a bit anticlimactic to just stop one day, without even trying. It's not like I overcame anything - I didn't defeat bulimia. I just grew tired of it and burned out on it. One day I just became normal. Never again did I have bulimia and there was not one slip up. Now, 30 years later at age 60, I am still healthy!

I hope you do not put down the book, disgusted and angry, thinking, "I read all of these pages to find out the cure, and the answer is to burn out and get tired of having bulimia? What a waste of my time!" Even though this part seems anticlimactic, honesty can be disappointing. We still have much to examine, more helpful ideas and some philosophizing to do, and my hope is that either my words or my experiences come back to you at a later time and help you through your difficult situations.

Looking back, I can see where going on a honeymoon gave me a reprieve from thinking about binging or buying any groceries and helped break my eleven year habit, and now I understand why staying at a hospital thirty-some years ago might have been the therapy I needed. Mom was right, as usual! It seems I was given just enough of a boost from several areas of my life improving, that I was content enough even with horrid skin to break free from bulimia. Not every portion of my life improved - and yet I was cured, and my mind was deprogrammed and reset at normal.

It is a pity I went through eleven years with an illness. The fears I had over those years were unfounded: afraid to eat normally, afraid I would not get to eat what I wanted, afraid I would get fat, and afraid I would be hungry. All the angst was a waste of energy, of time, money and health. All that isolation, binging and purging for fears that did not have to be fears at all.

CHAPTER FIFTEEN

THE LONG TERM EFFECTS

For several years after the bulimia ended I worried about going back to the same places I lived when I had bulimia, such as the Denver area, Detroit or Petoskey. I was afraid the same environment would make me repeat the old behaviors. Fortunately, once the urges left, they never returned.

Loneliness is bulimia's best friend and my worst enemy. That said, even as a healthy person, I have never been one to have a lot of friends. That is okay! Aloneness and loneliness have two different meanings and outcomes. It is fine to have a few friends and also enjoy being by yourself.

There is a saying that you have to experience bad times to appreciate the good times. It seems as if that is true. I love being by myself and I trust myself now. I look back with sadness at my past. Bulimia attached onto my life as a parasite and affected so many years, with wasted opportunities for relationships, success and happiness.

I remember how much I wanted to be normal, but immediately thought if I ate normally, I would get fat. When I finally got over bulimia I was very surprised to discover I could eat an occasional huge deli sandwich or a Hot Pocket and not gain weight. People with normal diets certainly can gain weight because there is such a variety in what constitutes a "normal diet," but it is possible to eat what is thought of as "normal food" and still maintain your weight. Besides, most former bulimics came out of bulimia with a great knowledge of calories, and we can eyeball just about any food and know how much to eat, and how much to cut back the next meal if we overeat. We are well-educated on the subject of food!

A long-term effect of having an eating disorder is how we think friends and family perceive us. It seems to me that those who knew me when I was pretty and successful and then found out about the eating disorder do not trust me anymore. Most of my friends and relatives are wonderful, warm and forgiving people, but in my head, my reputation has been ruined for life. I also have no idea how many other people have been told about my illness. Do my aunts and uncles know? Do friends of friends know? I have to just accept that it is normal for people to tell other people, and that these are the consequences of having such an unusual illness.

Ever since I developed the disorder, I have dreaded the idea of someone bringing up my past bulimia in a conversation. It seems like it would be so humiliating and embarrassing. Yet, once the conversation got underway, it probably would be easier than expected. This large chunk of my past still controls me, in a way, since it affects how I think others perceive me, so I am trying to take the next step toward being open about my past illness and be able to talk about it to anyone who asks, even with people from my past. My problem has always been anxiety about direct confrontation, and I want to conquer that fear too!

Even though bulimia had a connection to me being self-conscious, I became bulimia-free when I still had acne. Somehow, I learned to be strong enough not to let disappointment about my face keep me from participating in society, although, to this day, I avoid getting close to people and am embarrassed about my skin. I have just learned not to hide all together.

In the fall of 1989, well over two years after my bulimia ended, I attended my fifteen year high school reunion. A classmate came up to me, looked at my face, made a loud gasping sound and then blurted out: "What happened!" That sure felt like a valid excuse to hide, but I continue to this day to try to find the humor in everything and not get upset, because getting upset does no good. A similar experience occurred at my 40th high school reunion. I was emcee and gave my usual "cheerleader" rousing speech! Later, an old friend came up to me and surprised me, because I did not think he was coming to the reunion. He looked at me from a close range and then slowly put his head down before looking at me again, and I could detect disappointment. My acne had cleared up by this time, but the scars and large pores required a lot of makeup and even then they were not totally camouflaged, so I was not "the girl next door" anymore. It saddens me to disappoint others, but life leaves its battle scars and we must rise above them as best we can.

Another lasting issue with bulimia is how I see myself when I look back in life. Although I did some good deeds, had some wonderful experiences and worked hard at jobs, I cannot say I was a good person. I did not respect myself or like myself – certainly I was not proud of myself. How I perceive my behavior in the past is not something I can change with a positive attitude, because I consider it fact. I was not a good person. There was the good person inside, trying to get out, but my behavior was not worthy of the title "good." All I can do is be the best I can be at the present moment and always make wise plans for the future.

Could I have gotten over bulimia faster if I spent more time dealing with my personality? I think so. If you have a similar personality to mine, where you are timid toward much of life and are bulimic, the suggestions of getting out and participating in society will be contrary to what you want to do! You have to figure out the best way for you to get well, and that means working with more dedication and strength than the part of yourself that does not want to get well! I truly believe there is an answer for every bulimic; after all, we all were healthy once and our systems evolved to take in food and let it nourish our bodies, so that is the norm. What I also realize about my eating disorder is that if I went back in time, I would tackle this illness with much more determination. As the old saying goes, "Hindsight is 20/20!"

One more effect of bulimia was lingering, and I did not recognize it. Although I never starved myself, I still tried being thin and took off too much weight a few times. The last time I became too thin was after I remarried and wanted to get rid of the "fat roll around my stomach." I went from my normal weight which is around 116 pounds down to 105 pounds. There still was a little fat around my stomach and the rest of me looked too thin. However, in my eyes, I did not look too skinny. It was my husband who pointed out my bony frame, saying he could feel my ribs and that my hip bones were protruding. He said he liked me better with more weight on. That is always a hard comment for us to hear!

I disagreed with his opinion and would have tried to lose "just two more pounds," but one picture of me during Thanksgiving showed my entire body, and my legs slightly shocked me - it was clear that I was too thin. I had two choices: either I work out for hours to try to get rid of my tiny paunch, or I could accept that my body shape looks best with that mini roll around my tummy. I opted for the latter. Slowly, I reversed gears and put back on the eleven pounds I had lost, and I remember enjoying the process of gaining weight! The nice part is that I did not overeat or purge any food. Once the bulimia left, it never surfaced, no matter the circumstance.

CHAPTER SIXTEEN

WE CANNOT HIDE HERE

There is one place where most former bulimics are questioned: the dentist's office! We know we will be asked: "Do you grind your teeth at night?" We have to explain that the worn down teeth are due to bulimia and that it ended years ago. Even after stating that I have been healthy for thirty years, they ask, "Are you sure you are over it?" It is hard on the ego and the one locale your past is guaranteed to follow you if you were a binge-purge bulimic for several years, because the acids brought up by the purging wear down the teeth.

We have to accept their questions, because dentists still need accurate information for their records. There is an increased interest at the dentist's office that can make you feel a bit like a celebrity, because we are live specimens of what they studied in a textbook and they are interested in looking at our teeth! Two extra technicians came in to view my mouth at my first visit, after the dentist asked for my consent to let them take a look! Because of this disease 41-30 years ago, my teeth have almost no enamel on them. The dentist is always amazed I do not have pain and sensitivity as my teeth are very worn down, so in that respect, I am fortunate.

Like many former bulimics, several of my front teeth have been fixed and that was quite an expensive procedure. It took me a year to put away enough money to cover out-of-pocket expenses, even though I bought and used dental insurance wisely, keeping the insurance just long enough to make and permanently have new front teeth implanted in my mouth. Why did I get my front teeth fixed? By the time I was thirty, my front two teeth had been worn to the point I had only 2/3rds of their original length left.

Most former bulimics have all six top front teeth done, but I could only afford the front four. My dentist could not stand to see four new white teeth in the front and then my canines with that gray band at the top from the antibiotics I took in my younger days, so he filled in the tops of the canines at no additional cost, and now all six teeth blend and look natural. I am so thankful for the dentist's caring! There will probably be more crowns needed in the back of my mouth as the years go by, to fix all of my worn teeth.

Getting my front teeth fixed made a huge difference in my confidence level. In general, I am not a cosmetic surgery fan, but my new teeth allow me to give a real smile instead of the half-smile where I tried to hide the ends of my top teeth with my bottom lip and tried to hide the gray band at the top of my teeth with my top lip. It is worth all the pain of the procedure. I love being able to smile again!

CHAPTER SEVENTEEN

LIFE AFTER BULIMIA – NOT A PIECE OF CAKE

After the bulimia ended in 1987, I still had poor self-esteem, but I became a stronger person as the years went on. Some of the events that made me stronger were not happy ones, and I had to learn to constructively argue and stand up for myself. The reason I am telling you about the years after I was cured is that I do not want you to think all my problems went away and life became perfect when the bulimia ended! There still have been stresses, but I handle them without any urge to revert to my old ways of binging and purging.

All subjects need closure, and since I told you several areas where my life was lacking in quality, I will fill you in on some details, as it might help you look at some solutions to your own situations. Although my digestive system is healthy, I still have anxiety issues, obsessively worry about the littlest details and continue, at times, to hyperventilate. I have learned to manage the hyperventilation with techniques to keep the episodes mild, and both the anxiety and hyperventilation may be due to my three cups plus, per day coffee habit. Coffee has been a "safe drink" since I was a teen, because it has zero calories. I do love the taste! For the past few weeks I have cut down on my caffeine – again, and I have confidence I will keep it down to two cups maximum from now on, because I decided I want a slower heart rate for the sake of my health and to help lessen my anxiety. The decrease in caffeine seems to help. With all the worry, misuse of food, caffeine consumption, hyperventilation and anxiousness I have put my body through, I figure I have used up some heartbeats, and like anyone else, I want to have a long and healthy old age. Given the right motivation a long-term habit can be changed!

Just for the record, if I could go back to my college days and choose a career, I would either study Library Science or I would still try to get that Education degree, but major in Science, History or become a Reading Specialist. Those would be excellent careers for me, but I did not realize this in real time. I think I was too immature in several areas to settle down in a stable career.

One of my main problems was solved just seven years ago. At age 53 my strong hot flashes from menopause subsided. Also, at age 53 I went vegan. One of these changes at age 53 (hormones settling down or going vegan) had an unexpected outcome – my acne cleared up! I do not know which caused the solution or whether it was a combination of both. Regardless, it is a relief! The scars and large pores will never totally disappear, but overall, I feel fairly normal and have had minimal acne and no cystic acne since 53 years of age.

Becoming vegan was something I had wanted to do for awhile, but I was very nervous about limiting my food in any way, because limiting foods did not work out so well in my youth! I am quickly recounting the process of my switch to the vegan regime, because there may be some clues to adaptability in this experience. I first tried being vegetarian, and this was surprisingly difficult this second time around. I drooled while going by fast food restaurants, or I went in for some fries and then sat there with a large plate of fries and felt sorry for myself while ogling everyone else's burgers.

I did not cheat on the vegetarian diet, but I felt I would not be able to stay on this diet much longer and would soon return to eating the typical American diet. Before I gave up, I decided to try a vegan diet just to say I was vegan for a few days. My rules were that this would be a "no pressure" experiment and that I could return to eating meat and dairy at any time. It took four days to go from loving skim milk and not liking soy milk, to loving soy milk and being happy I was off of watery, bitter skim milk. Cheese and eggs were rough to live without at first, but I managed, probably because I started out more of a junk food vegan and slowly ate healthier! Since I was eating vegan, I decided to look into how animals were raised on factory farms. After watching four factory farm videos, I knew in my heart I had to stay vegan for life. It has been over six years since I went vegan, and it has not made me obsess over food or do anything abnormal.

An odd discovery is that I used to drink 3-6 glasses of skim milk per day, but now I only use soy milk on my cereal, with an occasional ½ glass of soy milk to drink. I have tried to analyze why I was so addicted to the skim milk and not to the soy milk, but other than the fact that soy milk is a little thicker, I really do not have an answer.

The nicest thing about being normal after being a bulimic is that I can feel proud of myself for my accomplishments now. In fact, there have been no clouds of shame hanging over my life from 1987 to the present. Although I am like everyone else and occasionally say or do something I regret, overall I have liked myself for the past 30 years. It feels so good to like yourself! There are aids for self-esteem at your fingertips these days, with the Internet in almost every home and I am sure there are self-help books at your library.

Although you can look up support groups or basic information about bulimia, do not isolate yourself like people do who spend all day looking up everything in life on the Internet! It helps to get out and talk with other people and form connections in addition to your Internet discoveries. Of course, it is not mandatory to get out and socialize, as some people are more introverted. For the majority of people with bulimia, though, we isolated ourselves through the disease, and it can be a step in the right direction to get involved outside of the house.

CHAPTER EIGHTEEN

HANDLING THOSE URGES

You want to be normal. One reason you may feel miserable is because you are not the normal person you want to be. Can you imagine yourself healthy, talking with friends? Just close your eyes and try to picture two friends and you walking down the street, and you are totally healthy and "the ideal you." Are you picturing it? The friends do not have to be people you know, and you don't have to look like yourself. Just picture how "the ideal you" relates to friends while walking down the street. How do you see yourself? No matter who is in the scene with me, I always picture "the ideal me" the same way. I am talking, laughing and confident, with no worries, and my friends are laughing with me. I look young, and not exactly like myself, but the important part is that I am laughing with friends, relaxed and enjoying myself. That is what I picture. No one can be that way all the time, but it is who I must want to be.

My mom once told me to "Fake it until you make it." This could be good advice for a bulimic. Get out there and pretend to be the person you want to be. Act the part! Do the things you imagine yourself doing. This is something I personally learned watching a small town high school football game. The quarterback got very upset at a member of the opposing team, and swung at him. For some reason, they did not take the quarterback out of the game. He had to immediately get a grip on his emotions and shake off his anger, then think about the next play and execute it. I watched him execute plays, and keep trying after his teammates missed catching several throws. They finally had enough successful plays to win the game. So no matter what mistakes you make, and how mortified you are about what you did, you have to shake it off and keep going.

Acting the way we want to be is not easy. It takes bravery. I always instantly felt competition when I acted as good as I could be as an adult, because I felt other people were better at being "good people." It is probably true, but it is not an excuse not to be "your best you." We all have something special to contribute, whether we are introverted, extroverted or somewhere in the middle.

Several times I have been told: "Don't be so hard on yourself," but this is more complex than the words indicate. I had to learn to relax and rid myself of some of the anxiety that kept me looking for a release, and although I wanted to take full responsibility for my actions, I also learned not to blame myself for my disorder. It sounds contradictory, but blaming anyone including yourself is too negative; just acknowledge you have a problem and try to take your life in a good direction.

The technique of commanding your muscles before you get urges and repeating the commands to yourself a few times during the day is worth trying. Come up with whatever commands you want, such as "Don't move"; "Do not eat the cookies"; or "Do not eat more than two and a half cookies." Another mental note I thought might be helpful to repeat is, "I don't want to do it anymore." It is a re-programming of sorts. There has to come a point where you take over and are stronger than the urges.

There are methods to weaken the instant urges. When an impulse hits, immediately, try to relax and let anxiety go. Research shows that if you do ignore the impulse or control it by eating only a small amount, you will feel better than if you give in and eat a larger amount. So the food may taste good, but it does not make you feel better! If I went back in time, I would try to get myself to use portion control when urges hit, and then get out of the house, and praise myself if I succeeded. Positive reinforcement and praise are important.

Although I am cured of bulimia, I will truthfully say I never starve myself. People at my work skip breakfast and then get too busy to eat until 2:00 in the afternoon. That will never happen to me! My daily routine is to eat breakfast, a mid-morning snack, lunch, usually an afternoon snack or just three pieces of candy, dinner, and a bedtime snack. It sounds like a lot, but I just keep the fat content low and all is well.

In the present, when I feel like I want to eat something and realize it is too early, I use different techniques. First, of course, I try to tell myself, "It isn't time yet," and I drink a glass of water, which dulls the urge for a snack, and work on something that takes concentration. If the hankering does not go away, then I might open a can of green beans, artichokes, asparagus or some chick peas, do some exercises, brush my teeth, use some mouthwash, or eat a pickle (the sour taste can take away the desire to eat sweets). If it is time for a snack or if I just want something that feels like a snack, I will have some reduced fat crackers, pretzels or graham crackers with some coffee or herbal tea, or eat some dry cereal as a hand snack (Cocoa Puffs cereal can be a good snack as it is filling, lower in fat than most snacks and very satisfying – and it is chocolate)! Another filling snack is a piece of whole grain bread (I use nondairy bread) with jam and a warm drink. This type of bread is only 70-100 calories and is very satisfying, with fiber, and minimal fat. Don't forget the possibility of a fruit or even a fruit Popsicle.

There are many studies where people fill themselves up on carbohydrates like sweet potatoes, potatoes, bread, rice, pasta, popcorn, etc., along with vegetables and fruits and they lose weight. The culprit is what is customarily put on the bread, potatoes, rice, pasta or popcorn, which is usually fatty and higher in calories. As you can see, I do not worry about a little sugar. A sweet potato with a little brown sugar on it is very satisfying and so is that bread with jam!

During the weekday I have carrots for a snack, cut horizontally into circles and then heated and softened in the microwave for 3-4 minutes. Throw a little salt on them and they are a surprisingly tasty snack! At work, I even have a couple of lemon drops or some cinnamon candy to tide me over until lunch, because I can handle it! This is good news, because it could be you saying that one day – "I had a piece of candy, because I can handle it!"

Of course, the above paragraphs are written from the perspective of the "well and healthy me." The "ill me" would have taken the bowl of Cocoa Puffs, dumped sugar, brown sugar and/or honey on it, drown it all with whole milk, and eaten three more bowls of cereal, then purged it all. It takes awhile to get into our heads that a small snack is satisfying and is the right thing to do, and that we want to do the right thing.

Just to prove former bulimics are not afraid of sweet treats, one of my splurges is creamy cashew ice cream with non-dairy chocolate chips that are melted first so it forms a shell on the ice cream. Yes, I can handle it! One of the secrets to not feel guilty is to use a small bowl for the ice cream and then use the minimum number of chocolate chips to form a small shell on top.

My reasons for mentioning dietary information are that people do not have to starve to maintain their weight and carbohydrates are not evil. I joke that I am a carboholic, and it is one addiction I will keep! I just weighed myself so I could finish this sentence, and at 5 feet 4 ½ inches I am 114 pounds, the same height and two pounds lighter than my cheerleader picture in high school. I am extremely healthy with a total cholesterol level of 120, take no medication, have no arthritis or bursitis, and rarely have a cold. Therefore, even if you have been bulimic for many years it is possible for your body to bounce back, because your body wants to heal.

Most people put on some weight as they get older. If I gain a couple of pounds, I just cut back a little, increase my exercise, and wait because it takes time for weight to come off, and just when I think my weight will never decrease, those few pounds come off. Being slim is still important to me, but not crucial to my identity. It's just more comfortable. No longer do I obsess, or think if I am not at "the perfect weight," I am not the real me. I step on a scale once every few months, because I just don't think about the numbers anymore. Believe, me, I used to weigh myself every day! Time can change even the strongest habits.

What is important for you right now is finding what is right for you and realizing that in any form of therapy you may not be cured in one or two sessions. Your participation is crucial; stay hopeful! Do not let some missteps derail you from continuing to try your hardest to rid yourself of bulimia, because you will sabotage yourself! I speak from experience. Unless you want to wait and just hope that you burn out like I did, you need to make a strong effort to improve your life and get the motivation to try different methods to regain your healthy eating habits.

Do not get jealous of other people your age who seem to have it all together, with a boyfriend or girlfriend and a lucrative career choice. As they say, you don't know what any of those people are really going through, and their lives may not be as rosy as they look. But how good or bad their lives may be are not important, as you never want to wish worse luck on someone else just to make your own life seem better! Sometimes you just have to realize that things come to people at different times.

Not everyone has a girlfriend or boyfriend all the time, and some people don't even want one! I mention this because not only was I raised with the assumption I would have a boyfriend and then get married, but I am a mother and I know many girls go through wanting a boyfriend, to wanting to be rid of the boyfriend, to being without a boyfriend and feeling depressed that they don't have a boyfriend! It seems like an obsessive cycle. I wish teens could be content with themselves regardless of their relationship status. I also know that comparisons with other people are much more intense now, with pictures being shared all over social media sites.

Barbara Noon

Always remember that people do not discover what they want to do in life at the same age, so comparisons are not always beneficial.

CHAPTER NINETEEN

ARE YOU REALLY AN ADDICT?

The answer to whether we are addicts or former addicts seems obvious – of course we are! But we still use a lot of control, make choices and show restraint when we think we are powerless. When we go to the grocery store, we do not rip open the bag of chocolate candies in the aisle and start gobbling them down as fast as we can. We don't want to be gorging ourselves in front of children, and we know eating in a store is shoplifting and we would be caught. So, we subconsciously restrain ourselves and follow rules – until we get out to our car and are by ourselves. But you see my point. It is not that we are totally out of control. We just think we have no control!

We even restrain ourselves in restaurants. We may order a little extra food, but we don't shovel everything down, because we do not want to attract attention. We are still controlling our food, even if we don't realize it! Since we are not consciously thinking when we select a bag of candy but do not rip into it, I wonder if we automatically turn off the urges of our subconscious thoughts when we are in stores around candy. Is this a secret to bulimia – to find a way to turn off subconscious thoughts and urges? Do binging thoughts arise as subconscious thoughts first and then become conscious thoughts? I am above my head right here, and this is a question for a professional! It would be helpful to know if we can turn off a thought early in its genesis, but of course, it is better yet if we just do not think about binging, and the latter is the goal! A healthy person might think about an extra slice of cake but never seriously considers binging, and this reinforces the idea that much of binging is a habit.

Remember, there was a time when you ate normally. That never went anywhere; it just has been tucked in a back pocket. Something stops us from eating normally. We feel we are powerless, but we are still making choices. The light switch to binge and purge is flipped on and we feel the light is too overwhelmingly strong to turn off, even though we can flip that switch back off long enough to go to classes, work, etc. It seems as if our brains are playing tricks on us! Since the power is there to turn the switch off, we just need to figure out how to turn the switch off at will, and then keep it off. Perhaps by not desiring the light anymore, there may be no need for the light to ever be switched on again.

Bulimia can make so much of your life more difficult. I knew I was disappointing my roommates, my parents and my friends. Bulimia was a way to use binging and purging as a diversion from addressing other issues. It seems I would rather totally be trapped in my house with a serous eating problem than be a mediocre person facing some challenges in a normal life, because the eating disorder would get all the attention and be my scapegoat. As long as I kept the bulimia around, I would not have to address my few non-food issues in my real life. I was transferring the blame for my problems to my eating disorder. The bulimia had a purpose after all.

Bulimia was an escape, and it was a place where I had "no control." I wanted no control. It was a "giving up" of everything, and getting a lot at once. It was a break from reality. Now, most people claim bulimia is a way to have control, not give up control. I think it is both. We certainly control our environment with these secret binges, sometimes because we do not have control over our lives, but we also "go hog-wild" with the food. It does seem like sneaking and eating food is a show of defiance and of strength, because we lack strength elsewhere. The binging is an action, and it feels like we are taking action, because we can't make decisions or take action in other areas of our lives.

I also know I just wanted a lot of food and blocked thoughts about common sense or being honest, because I wanted all that good tasting food! It is also possible we just don't want anyone else controlling us. With bulimia, it is your own world, so you can make many mistakes without being held accountable or having your ego crushed by other people. Since I had no coping skills, bulimia was the way I coped. I also think it was a form of comfort.

Would such behaviors be categorized as a type of depression? I think so, but I do not know for certain.

For me, adult life was overwhelming and disappointing. I expected each day to be perfect and to feel happy all the time. But our minds do not work that way; we can be committed to being happy one moment, and some situation can instantly make us moody or we can just forget to stay happy! We need reminders and nudges to enjoy life as much as possible.

One of the holdovers from being bulimic is that I still occasionally dream I have overeaten and am looking for a place to vomit. In the dream, I always worry someone is going to catch me, and I am also very disappointed that bulimia is happening to me again. I feel such shame and I become terribly upset in my sleep. When I wake up I am so thankful it is just a dream and I am fine! I hope someday these dreams will cease, but at least they are dreams and not reality! Do not worry about the bad dream though; just because this occasionally happens to me does not mean you will have any bad dreams that bulimia has returned.

Since I am on the subject of sleep, I have a tip that works for me when it comes to feeling better during the day. I have found that waking up early, even on weekends, keeps me from getting a headache, and when I get too much sleep I feel groggier. These are revelations that took me a long time to figure out, because most people will tell you to sleep in and get a lot of sleep! It just does not work well for me. Some people say sleeping with consistent hours is the key to feeling good. Since I have not looked into this subject and did not research depression during the entire time I was bulimic, all I can tell you about sleep is what works for me.

Just recently I noticed an important clue as to why the bulimia lasted so long in my case. I worried and obsessed and anguished, but what I did not do was set out detailed plans, with people to help me. I must have wanted to keep the option open to binge. I know it was because the urge was still strong, I loved all those sweets, and I feared eating normally.

It could be that I also kept the option open because, as long as I allowed the possibility that I might not succeed, I would not totally fail myself if I did binge. If I set myself up to succeed and then binged, it would feel hopeless. It makes sense from the standpoint of protecting my feelings, but, by not giving 100% of my effort, I could not be successful in ridding myself of bulimia. If I became hopeless from binging when I planned to succeed, I still would have to try another day. Therefore, trying to succeed with a full effort still seems like the best choice.

Perhaps I should have kept a notebook where I wrote down what the immediate plans would be for eating tomorrow, looking into careers, finding friends, being confident, and for sorting out my feelings. I've discovered insight into my own bulimia while writing this book, so writing can be helpful.

The fact that I never did write anything down makes me wonder if I actually was fooling myself about wanting to be cured. I felt destitute, cried buckets and thought I wanted to get rid of bulimia, but since the desire to keep eating whatever I wanted was so strong, I bet my psyche was never serious about getting rid of the illness.

If you do start writing plans, I would advise against counting calories or writing down foods you ate. We want to be normal, and writing down what we ate when we know we will eat too much is just shaming ourselves, and in my opinion, it might cause more harm than good. If any expert, a therapist or otherwise, tells you to write down your calories, or disagrees with my opinions in any way, go with what the experts say. I just think about what I would try and would not try if I still had the illness. I do think writing some positive goals of how you are going to improve your eating might be beneficial, or you could write down what went wrong and how you feel, as long as it does not depress you. You will have to judge whether it would be cathartic and freeing or whether it would bring your mood down.

Another idea might be to write stories or blog about non-food subjects as blogging can become a passion! It can be a release of creativity and feelings, and can keep you enthused. It would probably not be a good idea to write a blog about your bulimia, at least until you are over it, because you could open yourself up to hurtful comments and you may be sorry you made your illness public. It is important to find passions outside of food.

The most popular treatment for bulimia is behavior modification and out-patient therapy, as in going to the hospital for therapy but leaving when the hour is over and remaining in your own life. If someone does offer to pay for a total hospital stay as my mother offered for me, give it some careful thought. Do not outright reject it because of what the mental image implies. Perhaps visit where you might stay before you dismiss the idea. My bulimia may have ended several years earlier had I agreed to go to the hospital. Staying full-time in a hospital is not common though. There are many options to manage or cure your bulimia at select hospitals, with day stays, evening meetings or weekly visits. It looks like bulimia is now treated according to your needs and schedule.

It does bother me a bit that I could be right on the edge of having any type of mental disorder and not know it. It was a fine line between being healthy and becoming very ill when I took that first bite of the Heath bar. I did not know I would become bulimic, I did not try to become bulimic and I did not want to become bulimic; yet it plagued me for eleven years. Anything could happen to my brain at any time! Yet, I am so much stronger now, and I know that my life is two-thirds over, so it is more precious to me to live it as a mentally strong and healthy person. Integrity has become important to me. Not everyone can be proud of themselves for being normal, but once bulimia is conquered, you may find that you are very proud of yourself!

What I want to stress to current bulimics and their families is, if I were to make a list during the time I was bulimic and also right now of what is important in my life, food would not be on either list. Certainly, I do and did like eating, but cherished memories are about good times such as being with friends or family, playing horseshoes with grandpa, bicycling, researching subjects I am curious about, going to a museum, enjoying nature, petting my dog or doing crafts. These are so much higher on my list than eating, because I can't tell you what I ate three days ago, but I can remember the feel of my three year old son's hand in mine as we walked to the playground. (He is 23 now.) You as a person are so much more than just a bulimic, but the bulimia overwhelms you, and can keep you from the things that are important to you. Bulimia truly is a very small part of "who you are," and someday it will be a very small part of "who you were!"

A few months ago, I told a couple of friends online about my past problems with bulimia, and they surprisingly were very understanding and replied not to be ashamed about having a mental illness. One called it a psychiatric disorder, which was the first time I heard that term, and I embraced it and used it in this book. It made me feel better to be categorized as having a psychiatric disorder, because it shows something did go wrong with my brain that I could not help with my sick brain! The title "psychiatric disorder" is not an excuse, but it does give a bit of comfort to take the tremendous load of: "All of this is my fault," and chalk a little of it up to, "I had a psychiatric disorder, a mental illness." I don't think it is a cop-out as I still take responsibility, so somehow, both blaming myself and not blaming myself can co-exist!

Another difficulty we have with eating - what is normal? How do we eat normally, with all the different foods and diets, and doctors giving varied advice about what is good and what is bad for us? There truly is not one normal, since culture, availability and how you were raised plays a part in dictating what foods are in your cabinet. I have personal answers that I think are best when it comes to eating, but this book is not about clean arteries or extremely low cholesterol. It is about handling any food that comes your way, and being okay when you do eat a little too much. Food is a necessity to figure out as you go through life, but there is a difference in scale between healthfully watching what you eat, and being overtaken by what you eat.

People with eating disorders need to learn be able to eat a small sweet without flipping-out. In my bulimic years, if I refused a cookie in the presence of a roommate, there was a thought/plan in my head to binge as soon as I was alone. This is where some self-discipline should have come in. I should have accepted just one cookie to see if I could keep it down and to see if I visibly gained weight from it, but really I was just too ill and so afraid that I did not think of trying it. Eating one cookie shows some self-control, some enjoyment and is a positive plan that can bring pride to a bulimic. The saddest part about this eleven year ordeal is that I always could have had one, two or even three cookies or some gravy or an occasional handful or two of potato chips and I would have been fine. The needle on the scale would not have moved. There was no reason to binge and purge or fear food at all.

CHAPTER TWENTY

LEADING UP TO THE PRESENT

As time goes by, you may acquire more insight into your illness, just as the "whys" came to me very slowly. After reading some experts' opinions on the relationship between the lengths of time people have bulimia and the odds of curing it, I consider myself lucky. According to them, the sooner you become bulimic, the easier it will be to get over it, which makes sense. Certainly, it will save a lot of heartache if it is treated early. But do not despair if you have had bulimia for several years. You can be healthy again. After all, I think we all would agree that my bulimia was pretty severe, and yet, here I am thirty years past my bulimic nightmare, and I am absolutely fine!

In searching the Internet about recovered bulimics, it said those who have had bulimia for a long time either relapse or just do not totally get over it. Somehow, I doubt I was the only person to beat the odds! It was disconcerting to read such a dismal prediction, but I think there will more success stories as time goes on. All I know is I was not included in any polling about bulimia and I am a success story, so there may be a lot of us long-term bulimics who successfully conquered this illness years ago and just never reported it to anyone!

Some people think bulimics are starving themselves and need nutrients, but I know I was not that type of bulimic. I always made sure I had good food put into my stomach after my binges. Bulimia is not a "one size fits all" illness! There are so many variations of bulimia, I probably am not addressing the occasional bulimic, the anorexic bulimic, the male bulimic, or a bulimic who takes diuretics. Hopefully, if you fall into these different categories you have still bonded with my story enough that you don't feel so isolated, and are picking up some useful ideas!

When I think deeply about my experience with bulimia, there can be surprising revelations. It came to me that I never tired for long of binging and purging on the same foods, and even though I would say that this "one last binge" would satisfy my desire for a certain candy bar or for caramel syrup on ice cream, it never did. A day or two later, I could binge on the same type of candy bar and eat ice cream with caramel syrup again. I should have realized if I loved the taste of certain foods and binged on them and purged, and in one more day I wanted to binge on them again, then what was the value of those foods if they didn't satisfy my desire for them? It would be a never-ending cycle of eating those foods. There was no way to get well by having that "one last binge" because you will want more binges just like it. The satisfaction of one binge is very short-lived. At some point, there has to be a cutting-off point, even if you want to eat more of an item.

Is bulimia a lazy person's way to passion? It certainly is a displaced passion, as the energy should be used elsewhere. In my case, I feel the word "lazy" suits my behavior, as well as the word "impatient." Now that I am well, I find passion in many parts of life. A quote I have on my wall at work that I like to live by is: "A man who dares to waste one hour of time has not discovered the value of life." (Charles Darwin) This does not mean run around and try to be the craziest you can every minute, but instead enjoy and use your time wisely, and even cherish your time relaxing.

The advice I want to give people after being bulimic for so many years is to try everything when it comes to a cure! Give it your full commitment and give it time to work. The more effort you put into being cured and the less you give up, the sooner I think you will be over it. At first, it may seem like you are devoting too much time to thinking about food, something on which you are tired of focusing, but all the work will be temporary - until you break the bulimic habit and establish a new, more confident life.

Your goal is to be stronger than the "binging self" who has that desire to overtake you. Sometimes this becomes a tug-of-war that the "real self' needs to win, but sometimes the tussle is not necessary because the binging self just fades away as you find a healthy life more rewarding than binging. By having a more fulfilling life and a stronger real self and not rewarding the binging self, you starve the binging self until it disappears! (Please note I am using the word "starve" symbolically and do not mean for you to starve yourself!)

In reading over my ideas and tips, I feel odd suggesting that you work so hard at getting well, when my recovery happened automatically. However, I spent eleven long years chained to this illness, and some strong constant effort on my part was what was missing to end the illness sooner.

In the beginning of the book, I posted a picture of me as a cheerleader and I later said I might have needed more of a cheerleader-type counselor to motivate me. We all could use some kind of cheering on, but I do not know where a person will get this type of counseling. I thought about life coaches, motivational speakers and personal trainers, and they could be helpful, even though most are not experts in bulimia and should not take the place of a qualified counselor. Hopefully, you can find the type of motivation you need, even if it means you have a combination of counselors and motivators!

Now that you have read this book, if you are a bulimic, there is a chance you will react to it by binging and purging. After all, you will want to show yourself just how bad your bulimia is, and your brain may produce strong urges, which is a defensive reaction by your "binging self" because it does not want to be extinguished.

I hope I am wrong about the binge, but no matter what happens, do not give up! Make yourself an active part of your recovery. Get enthused about the idea of being well!

Whether you are bulimic, a family member or someone interested in the topic, I hope you have gained insight into the mind of a bulimic. If you have a son or daughter or friend with bulimia, it is my suggestion to try to help that person, even if he or she resents you for it, and chances are that will happen, in the short term. When I was a bulimic, I could have used stronger help; and since we know that people with bulimia will try to avoid being helped, having you ignore their problem will be just what they want. They need support. At the same time, never feel you must aid them, as each situation is different and you must be guided by what you feel is best for you, as well as for your loved ones.

If you have bulimia, hopefully you have found some useful ideas to try, and have been heartened by reading a success story. I wish you joy, confidence, a spark for life, and the desire to win the battle of bulimia. Once you identify what your own issues are, you can go from there with a determination to end this disease, rather than let it fester longer. Help yourself by getting help, and know that you are worth it!

The End

63307236R00074

Made in the USA
Lexington, KY
06 May 2017